LET'S GO
BUDGET

LONDON

Research Manager
Linda Buehler

Managing Editor
Chris Kingston

Editor
Spencer Burke

Contents

Discover London

Most people have a well-defined idea of "London"—staid tradition, afternoon tea, heavy ales, and cultured accents in tweed. People with this notion of London can easily complete their vacation in 3min. by making their way to the banks of the Thames and staring pointedly at the gilded heights of Big Ben, but this would be to miss the true charm of this expansive, diverse place.

Despite its weighty history, the city today is not all ghost tours, beefeaters, and double-decker buses. Beyond Buckingham Palace and the blinding lights of Piccadilly Circus, London is a living, breathing metropolis, home to more people than any other city in the European Union. Comprised of 32 boroughs along with the City, London can seem at times more like a conglomerate of villages than a unified city, but each part's unique heritage and character contributes to the big picture. Thanks to the feisty independence and diversity of each area, the London "buzz" is continually on the move—every few years a previously disregarded neighborhood explodes into cultural prominence. Wander between immigrant neighborhoods in East London, take part in a political rally in Trafalgar Square, and watch the Olympics return to the city for a third time. Each day in London brings something new, so finish up your pint and Let's Go!

Budget London

HAVE YOUR JELLIED EELS AND EAT 'EM TOO

Don't worry, you don't need to resort to eels to eat cheaply in London.

- ▶ **PIE MINISTER:** This punny pie shop offers some of the best English eats in the city at some of the best prices; it's sure to leave you satis-pied (p. 84).

- ▶ **FRANCO MANCA:** Order an individual pizza at this South London pizzeria. It's just like stepping through a wormhole to Naples (p. 95).

- ▶ **CITY CÀPHÊ:** Vietnamese *bánh mì* is your best bet for a delicious, cheap sandwich in the City (p. 79).

- ▶ **FREEBIRD BURRITOS:** We used to say it was impossible to find a good burrito in London. Then we found Freebird (p. 81).

- ▶ **LE MERCURY:** This is one of the best values in London; proof that good French food doesn't have to be expensive (p. 93).

A HOSTEL FIT FOR THE QUEEN

It can be hard to find budget accommodations in this notoriously pricey city. Good thing we've got you covered.

▶ **PALMER'S LODGE:** This refurbished Victorian mansion (once home to a biscuit magnate), is one of the highest-rated hostels in the city (p. 42).

▶ **CLINK 78:** Ever wanted to sleep in a jail that you could check out of? This expertly renovated old jail and courthouse is a great place to make your dreams come true (though the "cells" aren't for the claustrophobic) (p. 40).

▶ **ASTOR HYDE PARK:** Where else can you find hostel rooms with French windows and domed glass skylights? Aged grandeur and comfort mark this flagship of the Astor chain (p. 36).

▶ **ST. CHRISTOPHER'S VILLAGE:** A proud party hostel with lots of amenities, organized activities, and local character (p. 35).

Freebies

If you know where to go, it's possible to see some of the best London has to offer without paying a pound.

▶ **MUSEUMS:** Most of London's famous museums, including the British Musuem, Tate Modern, and the National Gallery, are gloriously free.

▶ **OLYMPICS:** Catch some Olympic glory for free at one of the free events, such as the marathon, triathlon, and cycling road race (p. 116).

▶ **EVENSONG:** Skip the ticket price and go to Westminster Abbey (p. 56) or St Paul's (p. 47) during Evensong. Just don't be a jerk and leave halfway through the service.

▶ **PARLIAMENT:** Instead of paying 15 quid for a tour, see democracy in action at a debate or committee session (p. 57).

PINCHING PENCE

London may be one of the most expensive cities in the world, but armed with the right guide (this one) you can experience much of what it has to offer without having to pawn the family jewels.

▶ **TAKE THE TUBE:** Unless you're up to walking a marathon each day, the Tube will be your cheapest way of getting around. Plan efficient journeys to save money. The Piccadilly Line, which runs between Central London and Heathrow, is the cheapest way to get to and from the airport (p. 144).

▶ **OYSTER CARDS:** Get a reusable Oyster Card and save your-self up to 50% on all London public transportation. You can also buy 1- and 3-day passes, or weekly, monthly, and annual Travelcards that give you unlimited rides (within specific zones) for their duration (p. 144).

▶ **SKIP SPECIAL EXHIBITIONS:** London's incredible free muse-ums are big enough that you'll have plenty to see without shelling out for the special exhibits.

▶ **SKIP TOURISTY SPOTS FOR SIMILAR, FREE ALTERNATIVES:** For example, instead of going to the kitschy Tower of London (nearly £20), get your history on at the Museum of London (free).

What To Do

MUSEUM HEAVEN ON EARTH

Luckily for budget travelers, many of London's world-class museums are completely free. Though there are countless great options, here are four that are unmissable. The **British Museum's** (p. 70) mind-blowing collection, ranging from the Elgin Mar-bles to the Rosetta Stone, will show you the full power of the British Empire. After that crash course in Western civilization, get another on Western art at the **National Gallery** (p. 53). The **Victoria and Albert Museum** (p. 63) contains design exhibits on all cultures and time periods. Finally, the **Tate Modern** (p. 60) will show you all the big names of 20th-century art—including

Duchamp, Pollock, and Warhol—and have you wondering just what is going on in a lot of the works. And you can simply stroll into all of these museums without paying any admission fee.

HOLD THE WHOLE WORLD, IN YOUR STOMACH

Other than admiring the relics in the British Museum, the best way to experience the legacy of the British Empire is to tour London's many delicious ethnic eateries. The city is brimming with great Indian food, but **Durbar** (p. 88) in Notting Hill has been producing some of the best of it for 54 years. You can also fill up on spicy comfort food at **Negril** (p. 96), a great Afro-Caribbean joint in Brixton. Many swear that **Sufi** (p. 96) in Shepherd's Bush makes the best Persian food in the city, while **Mien Tay** (p. 95) has the best price-to-quality ratio of East London's many Vietnamese eateries.

TO BEER OR NOT TO BEER?

Feel like a challenge? Try counting all the pubs in London. Or, save yourself the time and just visit the best. **Dove** (p. 114) will make you feel truly English as you sample its local ales at a picnic table on the banks of the Thames. **Cask** (p. 103) can only be described as Beer Heaven. At **The Drayton Arms** (p. 105), you can enjoy your ale while watching a play in the black-box theater or curled up in front of the fireplace. And for a cool pub without pretension, grab a drink at **The Goldhawk** (p. 113).

BEYOND TOURISM

Ready to take a break from drinking Newcastle and counting churches? Get more involved with British culture by studying, working, or volunteering in London. You can legislate with a **Parliamentary internship** (p. 171), hustle as a paid fundraiser for **Greenpeace** (p. 167), or make the whole world your stage by studying acting at **Shakespeare's Globe Theatre** (p. 165).

Student Superlatives

▶ **BEST PLACE FOR MONK-Y BUSINESS:** Westminster Abbey (p. 56).

▶ **BEST PLACE TO GET ARSE-ACHE:** Shakespeare's Globe Theatre (p. 62).

▶ **BEST WAY TO REPLACE YOUR STAIR MASTER:** Climb to the dome of St Paul's Cathedral (p. 47).

▶ **BEST PLACE TO EAT A THREE-COURSE MEAL OF PIE:** Pie Minister on the South Bank (p. 84).

Planning Your Trip

To say that London is a sizeable city is to adopt the infamous British tendency for understatement. London is bloody massive. The central knot of museums, historical sights, shopping, and entertainment stretches along the Thames from the City of London (yes, a city within a city) through the West End to Westminster. The luxurious residential neighborhoods of Chelsea, Kensington, Notting Hill, and Marylebone lie to the north and west. Add in the university neighborhood of Bloomsbury and the culturally prominent South Bank and you've got the whole of central London in a nice package.

Now for the fun bits. With sky-high rents in the city center, the beating heart of city life has migrated a few miles out from the center. North London is the most upscale, East London is home to the city's hip and artsy, and South and West London are defined by their large immigrant communities (and great ethnic cuisine).

Navigating the sprawl of London can be incredibly frustrating. Fortunately, the ever-obliging Brits plaster the city center with maps, which can be found reliably at bus stops. If you don't want to leave your direction to chance, you can always out shell out for the all-knowing A-Z city map.

Icons

First things first: places and things that we absolutely love, sappily cherish, generally obsess over, and wholeheartedly endorse are denoted by the all-empowering ⬛ **Let's Go thumbs-up.** In addition, the icons scattered at the end of a listing can serve as visual cues to help you navigate each listing:

⬛	Let's Go recommends	☎	Phone numbers	⚲	Directions
i	Other hard info	Ⓢ	Prices	⏰	Hours

WHEN TO GO

The first thing to know is that, in London, just about any day of the year can be warm, cold, or extremely wet. That said, the summer months offer the best odds of at least not being cold and wet at the same time. Festivals like the Notting Hill Carnival and the BBC Proms help make July and August the liveliest months in the city. In 2012, the Olympics will be taking place from July 27 to August 12, so the city will be busier, livelier, and more expensive than ever for those two weeks. The low season (November through March) is when you can find the best deals on airfare and accommodations, so long as rainy (and sometimes snowy) weather doesn't cramp your sightseeing style too much.

NEIGHBORHOODS

The City of London

One of the oldest and most historic parts of London, the City of London, often referred to as "the City," is home to many of London's finest (and most crowded) tourist attractions as well as the city's financial center. The City holds many of London's Roman artifacts, including vestiges of the ancient London Wall. Next to these relics, the spires of famous churches are juxtaposed with the towers of powerful insurance companies. Many old buildings are marked by two of the city's most devastating tragedies: the Great Fire of 1666 (which destroyed 80% of the city in five days) and the German Blitz during WWII. The fantastic architecture that either survived these calamities or replaced the less fortunate buildings now stands as a monument to London's resilient spirit. As you head farther north, the City fades into **Farringdon** and **Clerkenwell,** which provide something of a buffer zone from East London. Here you'll find a mix of the yuppie-gentrified City and the hipster-gentrified East; somehow, this turns out to be a magical combination, producing quirky pubs and terrific food.

Reign, Reign, Go Away

Her Majesty the Queen may be the Head of State, but she doesn't own the place. Before entering the City of London, the Queen must respect London's sovereignty and greet the Lord Mayor of the City on its outskirts to ask permission to enter. We're all still wondering what happens if he says no.

The West End

The West End is one of the largest, most exciting parts of London. Its twin hearts are **Soho** and **Covent Garden,** but the neighborhood encompasses the area between Bloomsbury and the Thames, from the edge of Hyde Park to the City of London. Within that expanse are some of the city's best public museums (such as the **National Gallery** and the **National Portrait Gallery**), world-famous theater, interesting restaurants, loads of shopping, and vibrant nightlife. You can find just about anything you're looking for here (except maybe a good curry—Indian culture is strangely absent in this part of London).

Soho, most easily accessible via ⊖**Tottenham Court Road,** is one of the hipper and seedier parts of London. Home to one of the city's most prominent GLBT communities, Soho bursts at the seams with nightlife for gay and straight clubgoers alike. By day, this area (particularly **Chinatown,** located off Gerrard St.) is known for its excellent restaurants. North of Soho, **Oxford Street** is the capital of London shopping streets, with department stores and cavernous flagships of major clothing chains. Smaller boutiques and many salons can also be found in this part of town. To the south and west, the buildings get fancier and the streets are quieter in regal neighborhoods like **St James's.** All in all, the West End feels like one of the most touristy parts of the city, but perhaps that's because it so conveniently encapsulates what London is (deservedly) famous for.

Westminster

Westminster lays claim to the remainder of London's most famous sights unclaimed by the City of London. Between **Westminster Abbey,** the **Houses of Parliament,** and **Buckingham Palace,** Westminster still feels like the seat of the royal empire. Aside from these sights, though, there isn't much to do here. Nearby ⊖Victoria is a transport hub, surrounded by fast-food restaurants and touristy pubs. South of Victoria lies **Pimlico,** a residential neighborhood offering a few accommodations, many of them on Belgrave Rd. This area is also home to some higher-quality places to eat and drink.

The South Bank

This neighborhood is located in the south of Central London on, you guessed it, the south bank of the Thames. Populated with the renovated factories of yore, the South Bank has undergone a renaissance, reinforcing its status as a hub of London entertainment. This reputation didn't spring from nowhere: both the **Rose** and **Shakespeare's Globe Theatre** once stood here. Now, the **Southbank Centre** hosts classical music concerts, films, and more. There are also some of the best museums and galleries in London, including the famous **Tate Modern. Millennium Mile** stretches from the London Eye in the west eastward along the Thames, making for a beautiful walk, especially around sunset. More than just a cultural or aesthetic destination, the area around London Bridge and Borough is full of great pubs and restaurants with an eye on quality, perhaps thanks to the local **Borough Market.**

South Kensington and Chelsea

Kensington and Chelsea—excuse us, the Royal Borough of Kensington and Chelsea—is quite possibly the poshest part of London. And it knows it. The winding avenues and tree-lined side streets are full of mansions, columned townhouses, leafy gardens, and even royal residences. You'll know you're in the right place if you find yourself surrounded by nice suits, pearls, and the smell of money. High-priced restaurants are found alongside swanky cocktail bars and plenty of grand pubs. The shopping is to die for, and the museums are the city's best—and most are free. This is a big neighborhood—its geography almost as intimidating as its prices—extending roughly from Hyde Park Corner south to the river, and west all the way to Earl's Court.

Hyde Park to Notting Hill

Hyde Park is, we promise, actually a park. It's roughly rectangular with a Tube stop at pretty much every corner—**Marble Arch,** the incredibly unhelpfully named **Hyde Park Corner, High Street Kensington,** and **Queensway.** North of the park are a set of neighborhoods that get progressively nicer as you move west. Paddington, Edgware Rd., and Queensway mix fairly fancy houses on their back streets with main roads that have plenty of cheap ethnic eateries, souvenir shops, and stores of questionable legality that can unlock your phone, cash your checks, and wire your money across the world. Notting Hill has the mansions you would imagine, but popping out of the Tube at **Notting Hill Gate** may be a bit of a shock if you're expecting the set from a Julia Roberts movie—it's pretty much dull commercial real estate. Head slightly north, though, and you'll find the villas you were expecting. In the middle of that, **Portobello Road** has a market, antique stores, vintage clothing, and the kind of minimalist, hip cafes and restaurants that seem to appear anywhere you can get a secondhand prom dress or a pair of cowboy boots.

The Old Smoke

Paris is the City of Light. Rome is the Eternal City. London is the... um... sorry, what?

While other popular destinations proudly brand themselves and emboss glossy advertisements with catchy slogans, it's as difficult to discover London's nickname as it is to see the bottom of the Thames. On a related note, the term "The Old Smoke" is derived from London's notorious environmental issues. As commonplace and exasperating as the Cockney accent, industrialization and coal-burning caused air pollution, which in turn caused smog over the city. After the Great Smog of 1952, the government initiated efforts to clean up their act with the well-named Clean Air Act. Though the environmental outlook has altered, London's nickname hasn't yet. Probably because "The City Formerly Known as the Old Smoke" doesn't sound any better.

Marylebone and Bloomsbury

It doesn't get much more British than Marylebone—from the fact that Sherlock Holmes lived here to its mystifying pronunciation (it's *Mar*-leh-bone). Lush **Regent's Park** is surrounded by gleaming mansions, **Marylebone Lane** is lined with pubs, and the side streets are pocketed with clusters of Indian and Middle Eastern restaurants. The neighborhood stretches from Regent's Park south to Oxford St., and from Edgware Rd. east until it bleeds into Bloomsbury. While Marylebone is fun to poke around in, the prominence of fancy residential areas and spiffy office buildings means that good values here are hard to find.

Bloomsbury, on the other hand, is famous for its bohemian heritage. The namesake Bloomsbury Group included luminaries like Virginia Woolf, John Maynard Keynes, and E.M. Forster. Today, you can feel the continuation of all that cleverness emanating from the **British Library** and **University College London**—though creeping gentrification means there are few affordable garrets left for the burgeoning artist-intellectuals of today. Bloomsbury, centered on **Russell Square,** stretches east to King's Cross Rd., and is bounded on the north and south by Euston Rd. and High Holborn, respectively. The western part is now very high-end, while the eastern and northern bits retain more of the old student vibe. You can find some cheap pubs and restaurants throughout the streets surrounding the university, and the area is packed with good hostels, especially around **King's Cross**.

North London

North London is a sprawling expanse of fairly residential, but often quirky, neighborhoods. **Hampstead, Islington,** and **Camden Town** are the most popular draws. On the whole, north London is characterized by its gentrification, which has made the area safer without entirely depriving it of character. Hampstead provides pleasant dining and a proper small-town feel. Camden was once punk central, but it's now full of safety-pin-wearing 16-year-olds pretending that it still is. It also offers the glorious and meandering **Heath,** a must for all nature-lovers. Still worth a visit, Camden contains some underground culture and many upscale restaurants and boutiques. Islington is the easternmost part, quite pretty and residential but still with a bit of East London grit. Check out Upper St., which runs between ⊖Angel and ⊖Highbury and Islington, for great restaurants, bars, and shopping.

East London

Once upon a time, East London (and especially the **East End**) was considered a den of poverty and crime due to poor dock-workers and waves of immigrants who settled there over the centuries. You can see traces of the neighborhood's gritty past in the winding old lanes and thriving curry houses of **Brick Lane,** but it has slowly evolved into one of the most interest-ing parts of the city. The converted warehouse galleries and cutting-edge exhibitions attest to its popularity with artists. The hipsters and students who flocked to the cheap rents and underground cool factor have made it a haven for exciting and alternative nightlife (centered on **Shoreditch** and **Old Street**). The presence of immigrant communities mean that it's packed to the gills with cheap ethnic cuisine, and a new Overground line has made it more accessible than ever.

South London

South London has long been maligned as one of London's dodgier neighborhoods. While the area has enjoyed some-thing of a renaissance in recent years, it's still not as safe as much of central London. **Clapham** is a good place to find pubs and restaurants full of young professionals. Clapham has also become a cultural hub as the home of the **Battersea Arts Centre,** renowned for its groundbreaking productions. **Brixton** is less quaint, but a bit more fun. Bible-thumpers preach the Apocalypse from convenience store pulpits, and purveyors of goods set up shop at the nearby Afro-Caribbean market, despite the overpowering smell of fish. Brixton is the place to come if you've started missing fast food, though some truly excellent restaurants peek out from between the fried-chicken stands. At night, it's a popular place to hear underground DJs and live reggae shows. The local Underground stations across the south of the city play classical music, thought by many to be a tactic for keeping young people from accumulating in the Tube, *Clockwork Orange*-style.

West London

West London is one of the most shape-shifting parts of the city. **Shepherd's Bush** is a hub of ethnic life, evident in the varied restaurants lining Goldhawk Rd., culminating in the veritable World's Fair of Shepherd's Bush Market. Shepherd's Bush is also home to Westfield's, a 43-acre ode to consumerism that makes American strip malls look like rinky-dink corner stores. **Hammersmith,** the neighborhood to the south of Shepherd's Bush, is quieter and more gentrified. It feels more like a seaside resort than London—once you get out of the thriving area surrounding the Tube station, that is. Farther south and west are **Kew** and **Richmond,** which have the luscious greenery of Kew Gardens and Hampton Court, two easily accessible places to escape the urban jungle

SUGGESTED ITINERARIES

Cheap Date

Here's how to have an inexpensive, but romantic, night out in London.

> **1. HAMPSTEAD HEATH.** Take a relaxing stroll through **Hampstead Heath's** 800 acres (p. 73). You could easily pretend it's a walk in the English countryside. Then, climb Parliament Hill for one of the best views of the city.

> **2. LE MERCURY.** Head to nearby **Le Mercury** for an incredible French meal (p. 93). Impress your date with your intimate knowledge of the city's best eats at the best prices.

> **3. BLUES, BOOZE, AND BORDERLINE.** Head to the West End then hit up the "best blues bar this side of the Atlantic" at **Ain't Nothin' But** (p. 101), which has live music every night of the week (and £3.50 beer). If you need a beat to seal the deal, hit the dance floor at **The Borderline** (p. 100).

How to Spend a Very British London Sunday

To have an authentically British Sunday, you should start off with a gray sky and a temperature around 50° F (or, if you want to be really British, 10° C). Ideally it will be drizzling, then raining harder and harder as the day goes on. Though it's possible to continue this very British Sunday without the appropriate weather, you may feel like an imposter.

1. PORTOBELLO ROAD. Take the bus to Notting Hill. Walk down **Portobello Rd.** (p. 13) looking at the vintage stores and antiques markets. The narrow sidewalks and British manners will mean that every time you encounter another person with an umbrella, an awkward dance of "oh you pass first," "no, you go ahead" will ensue.

2. SUNDAY ROAST. Consume a ▨**Sunday Roast** at a cozy pub. *Let's Go* likes the slightly quirky take offered at **Coach and Horses** (p. 79) in the City of London. Learn to love the mushy vegetables like a real Brit.

3. MUSEUM. As the rain picks up, head inside one of London's many free museums. Feel properly imperial at the **British Museum** (p. 70), get cozy with Shakespeare at the **British Library** (p. 71), or see the men and women who built the country at **The National Portrait Gallery** (p. 54).

4. TEA AND THE BBC. Head back to your hostel, make yourself a cup of tea, and curl up with a book or the BBC. You're not going out tonight, because the rain is still thundering down. Everything's closed anyway.

A Three-Day Weekend in London

Day One

Head to Bloomsbury for two of London's best sights. The **British Museum** (p. 70) exhibits the spoils of hundreds of years of empire, including such famous pieces as the Rosetta Stone and the Elgin Marbles. Don't miss it. Have yourself an exceedingly English lunch at **Newman Arms** (p. 90). Just 15min. away is the **British Library** (p. 71), where you can see everything from the Magna Carta and Shakespeare's First Folio to Beethoven's tuning fork and the original, handwritten lyrics to "A Hard Day's Night." If you're a *Harry Potter* fan, **King's Cross Station** is next door. Take the tube into West London, and wander through the veritable World's Fair that is **Shepherd's Bush Market** (p. 15) for a taste of the city's ethnic diversity. For even more of a taste, head to **Sufi** (p. 96) for the best Persian food in London. End the night with a frothy pint on the banks of the Thames at **Dove** (p. 114).

Day Two

Start your second day with London's classic sights, clustered around the city's historical core, the City of London. Try stepping inside **St Paul's Cathedral** (p. 47) without exclaiming the Lord's name in vain. Climb to the top of the dome for an excellent view over the city's rooftops. Stroll through **The Temple** (p. 49), an incredible architectural hodgepodge best seen on the labyrinthine paths through the complex. Take a gander at the **Tower of London** and **Tower Bridge,** but don't bother paying to go inside. Have some lunch at **Clerkenwell Kitchen** (p. 80) or **City Càphê** (p. 79), then head down the river toward Westminster. Snap the requisite pictures of **Big Ben** and the **Houses of Parliament** (p. 57), then spend some time admiring the spiritual center of London, **Westminster Abbey** (p. 56). Walk up through **St. James's Park** to **Buckingham Palace** (p. 59) then cross the river for a dinner at **Pie Minister** (p. 84) followed by cocktails at **The Hide** (p. 104). If you're not already asleep on your feet, continue on to a blues show at **Ain't Nothin' But** (p. 101) or dancing at **The Borderline** (p. 100), both in the West End.

Day Three

The **Tate Modern** (p. 60) will make you repeat, yet again, "How can all these incredible museums possibly be free!?" While you're in the neighborhood, choose whether you're more interested in design or war (a tough decision, we know), and visit either the **Design Museum** or the **Imperial War Museum** (p. 61). Continue on to **Borough Market** (p. 135) and pick out a picnic lunch from the tangle of gourmet food stands under the old railway viaducts. Make your way to **Trafalgar Square** (p. 54) and conclude your museum tour of London with the **National Gallery** (p. 53). Get some dinner at **Shibuya** (p. 91), then bid farewell to London with a wild night out at the many excellent clubs in the **West End** (p. 100).

Planning Your Trip

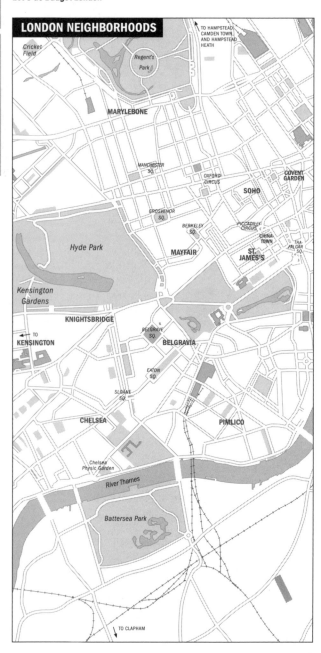

LONDON NEIGHBORHOODS

TO HAMPSTEAD,
CAMDEN TOWN,
AND HAMPSTEAD
HEATH

Cricket
Field

Regent's
Park

MARYLEBONE

MANCHESTER
SQ.

OXFORD
CIRCUS

COVENT
GARDEN

SOHO

GROSVENOR
SQ.

BERKELEY
SQ.

PICCADILLY
CIRCUS

CHINA
TOWN

TRA-
FALGAR
SQ.

Hyde Park

MAYFAIR

ST
JAMES'S

Kensington
Gardens

KNIGHTSBRIDGE

← TO
KENSINGTON

BELGRAVE
SQ.

BELGRAVIA

EATON
SQ.

SLOANE
SQ.

CHELSEA

PIMLICO

Chelsea
Physic Garden

River Thames

Battersea Park

TO CLAPHAM

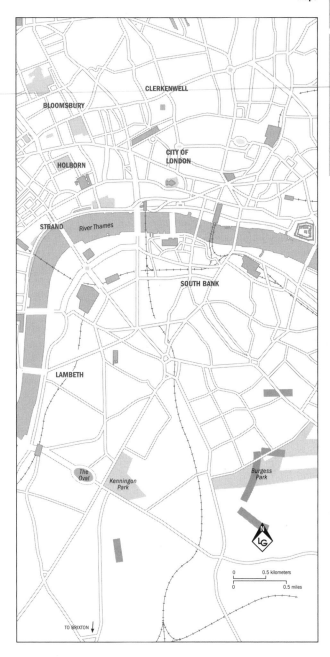

CLERKENWELL

BLOOMSBURY

HOLBORN

CITY OF LONDON

STRAND

River Thames

SOUTH BANK

LAMBETH

The Oval

Kenningon Park

Burgess Park

N

LG

0   0.5 kilometers

0   0.5 miles

TO BRIXTON

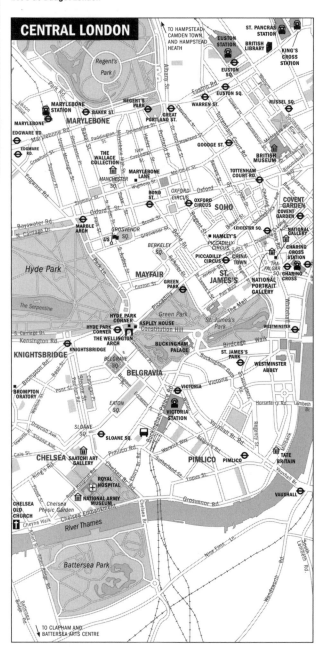

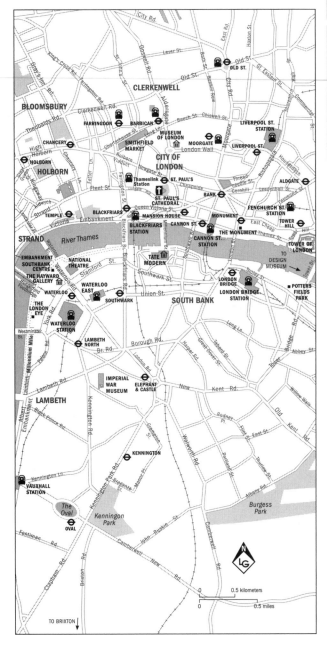

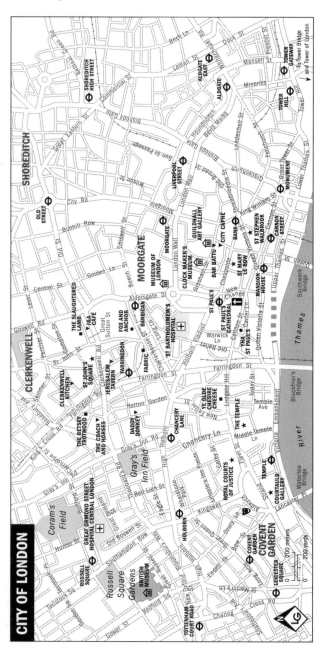

CITY OF LONDON

Planning Your Trip

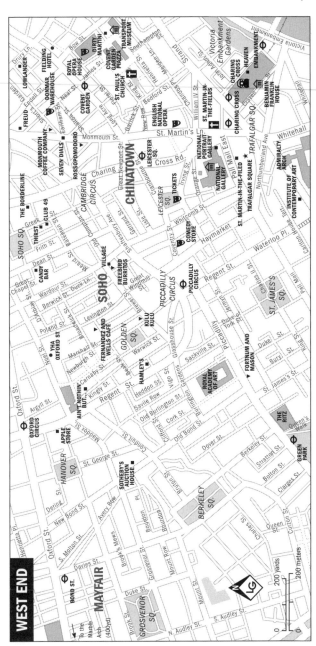

WEST END

MAYFAIR

SOHO

CHINATOWN

COVENT GARDEN

TRANSPORT MUSEUM

LOWLANDER

FIELDING HOTEL

FREUD

DONMAR WAREHOUSE

ROYAL OPERA HOUSE

DIRTY MARTIN'S

COVENT GARDEN PIAZZA

ST. PAUL'S CHURCH

MONMOUTH COFFEE COMPANY

SEVEN DIALS

ROSSOPOMODORO

ENGLISH NATIONAL OPERA

ST. MARTIN'S

ST. MARTIN-IN-THE-FIELDS

CHARING CROSS

HEAVEN

EMBANKMENT

BENJAMIN FRANKLIN HOUSE

NATIONAL PORTRAIT GALLERY

NATIONAL GALLERY

ST. MARTIN-IN-THE-FILED

TRAFALGAR SQUARE

ADMIRALTY ARCH

INSTITUTE OF CONTEMPORARY ART

LEICESTER SQ.

TICKETS

COMEDY STORE

THE BORDERLINE

THIRST

CLUB 49

SOHO SQ.

CANDY BAR

VILLAGE

FREEBIRD BURRITOS

KULU KULU

SOHO

GOLDEN SQ.

FERNANDEZ AND WELLS CAFÉ

AIN'T NOTHIN' BUT...

HAMLEY'S

PICCADILLY CIRCUS

FORTNUM AND MASON

ROYAL ACADEMY OF ART

ST. JAMES'S SQ.

THE RITZ

GREEN PARK

YHA OXFORD ST.

OXFORD CIRCUS

APPLE STORE

HANOVER SQ.

SOTHEBY'S AUCTION HOUSE

BERKELEY SQ.

BOND ST.

GROSVENOR SQ.

To the Marble Arch (400yd)

200 yards

200 meters

Piccadilly

Regent St.

Oxford St.

Charing Cross Rd.

Strand

Whitehall

Victoria Embankment

Waterloo Pl.

Haymarket

Pall Mall

Shaftesbury Ave.

Wardour St.

Dean St.

Frith St.

Greek St.

Berwick St.

Old Compton St.

New Bond St.

Conduit St.

Savile Row

Old Bond St.

Cork St.

Clifford St.

Bruton St.

Berkeley St.

Dover St.

Albemarle St.

Duke St.

St. James's St.

Jermyn St.

Bury St.

King St.

Carlton House Terr.

Northumberland Ave.

Pall Mall East

Garrick St.

Long Acre

Bow St.

Drury Ln.

Endell St.

Monmouth St.

Neal St.

Mercer St.

Bedford St.

Southampton St.

John Adam St.

King William St.

William IV St.

Cranbourn St.

Irving St.

Orange St.

Whitcomb St.

Coventry St.

Great Windmill St.

Brewer St.

Poland St.

D'Arblay St.

Marshall St.

Lexington St.

Beak St.

Carnaby St.

Kingly St.

Regent St.

Vigo St.

Burlington Gardens

Glasshouse St.

Sackville St.

Duke of York St.

Charles II St.

Queen's Walk

Stratton St.

Bolton St.

Clarges St.

Queen St.

Curzon St.

Charles St.

Mount St.

Brook's Mews

Grosvenor St.

Davies St.

S. Molton St.

Dering St.

St. George St.

Maddox St.

Mill St.

Heddon St.

Argyll St.

Great Marlborough St.

Noel St.

Newburgh St.

Warwick St.

Broadwick St.

Brook St.

Duke St.

S. Audley St.

N. Audley St.

Mount Row

Boyle St.

Aldford St.

Avery Row

Henrietta Pl.

Hanover St.

Great Newport St.

Earlham St.

Shorts Gardens

Mercer St.

Bedfordbury

Chandos St.

New Row

Victoria Embankment Gardens

Planning Your Trip

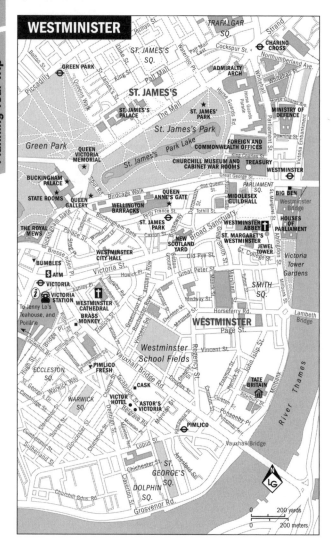

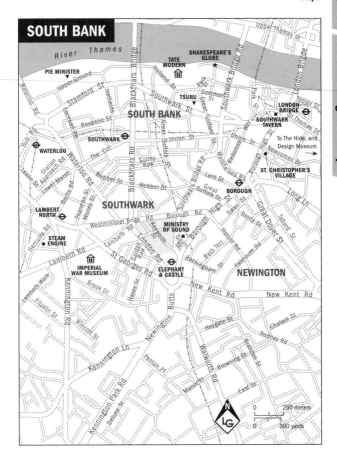

SOUTH BANK

River Thames

Upper Thames St

PIE MINISTER

Upper Ground

TATE MODERN

SHAKESPEARE'S GLOBE

Waterloo Rd

Stamford St

Hatfields

Blackfriars Bridge

Southwark St

Holland St

TSURU

Park St

Summer St

Bear Gdns

Clink St

Southwark Bridge Rd

Park St

London Bridge

Tooley St

St Thomas St

LONDON BRIDGE

SOUTHWARK TAVERN

SOUTH BANK

Roupelle St

SOUTHWARK

The Cut

Surrey Row

Union St

Great Guilford St

Marshalsea Rd

Borough High St

Newcomen St

To The Hide, and Design Museum →

ST. CHRISTOPHER'S VILLAGE

WATERLOO

York Rd

Station Approach Rd

Waterloo Rd

Lower Marsh

Baylis Rd

Webber St

Blackfriars Rd

Webber St

Great Suffolk St

Southwark Bridge Rd

Lant St

Long Ln

BOROUGH

Tabard St

Great Dover St

Trinity St

Swan St

SOUTHWARK

LAMBETH NORTH

Hercules Rd

Westminster Bridge Rd

Morley St

Pearman St

Lambeth Rd

Borough Rd

MINISTRY OF SOUND

Borough High St

Harper Rd

Falmouth Rd

STEAM ENGINE

Lambeth Rd

London Rd

Gaunt St

Gaywood St

St Georges Rd

Rockingham St

Bath Terr

NEWINGTON

IMPERIAL WAR MUSEUM

Lambeth Walk

Kennington Rd

Brook Dr

Hayles St

Butts

ELEPHANT & CASTLE

New Kent Rd

New Kent Rd

New Kent Rd

Fitzalin St

Wincott St

Newington

Heygate St

Chatam St

Rodney Rd

Kennington Ln

Penton Pl

Walworth Rd

Browning St

Beaconsf St

Kennington Park Rd

Dedtunp St

Manor Pl

East St

N

LG

0   200 meters

0   200 yards

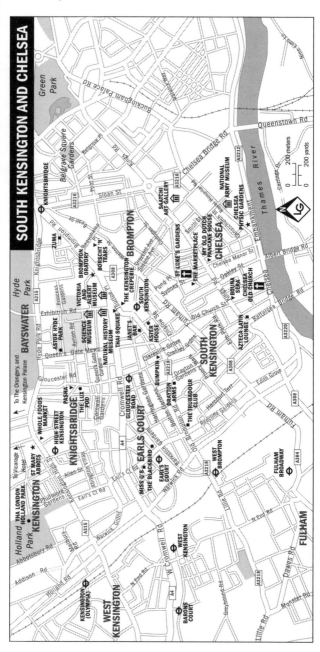

SOUTH KENSINGTON AND CHELSEA

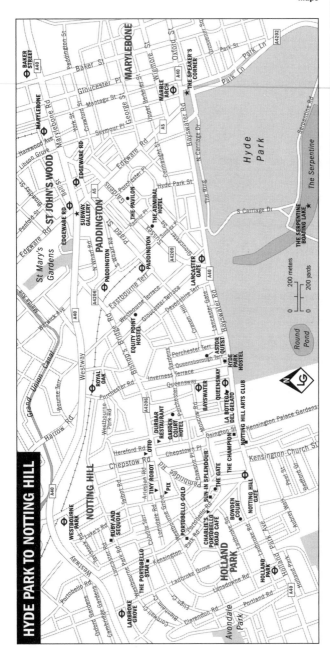

HYDE PARK TO NOTTING HILL

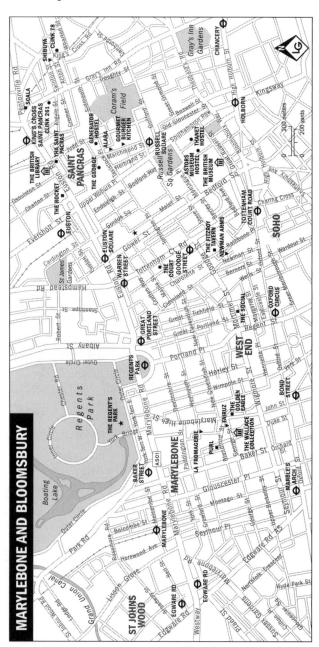

MARYLEBONE AND BLOOMSBURY

Accommodations

London is an infamously expensive city, and its accommodations are no exception. Standard London hotels almost always come with astronomical price tags (for an exception, see East London's Hoxton). But there are many excellent hostels, especially in Earl's Court, the area north of Hyde Park, and Bloomsbury (extra emphasis on Bloomsbury). In most neighborhoods, you can choose between party hostels with late-night bars and organized pub crawls, and quieter ones with more sedate guests. Travelers looking for long-term lodgings should look into renting college dorms during the summer. You can also find short-term rentals online (www.gumtree.com is a good place to start), which can save you precious pounds. Keep in mind that many hostels also offer private rooms. For those unwilling to stay in a hostel, guest-houses and bed and breakfasts are much more reasonable. Many pubs also rent rooms on their upper floors. Though these smaller establishments still aren't exactly cheap, they tend to offer a good value for their high quality.

Budget Accommodations

If you're the kind of traveler who views hostels as dirty, scary places, you're going to have to face your fear. London has few mid-range accommodations options, so you're generally choosing between budget hostels and pricey hotels. Fortunately, in a city this large, hostels come in every shape, size, and scent. More often than not, hostels will be just as clean and classy as a hotel, for half the price. Hostels are all around the city, but head to Bloomsbury for the best variety. If you insist on having a private room, the area between Hyde Park and Notting Hill is your best bet.

THE CITY OF LONDON

YHA St Paul's — HOSTEL $

36 Carter Ln.

☎0845 371 9012; www.yha.org.uk

We don't know how they managed to squeeze a budget hostel into the heart of the City, but somehow they did. This YHA outpost is housed in the former school for St. Paul's choir, a splendid old stone building just across from the cathedral. Rooms are clean and modern with useful amenities, like en-suite washbasins and desks. There's a lounge and dining area available, and although there's no kitchen, an on-site restaurant does serve meals. The staff organize events and tours of the city. Check the list of upcoming concerts on the blackboard by reception.

▶ ⇆ ⊖St. Paul's. Go right down New Change, turn at the cathedral onto Cannon St., then take a left onto Carter Ln. *i* Breakfast available. Laundry facilities available. All dorms single-sex. Wi-Fi available in the lounge and some rooms; £1 per 20min., £5 per day., £9 per week. $ 4- to 11-bed dorms £15-25; singles £20-35; doubles £41-74.

Fox and Anchor — HOTEL $$$$

115 Charterhouse Sq.

☎0845 347 0100; www.foxandanchor.com

The six rooms on top of this elegant pub are what a Victorian gentleman's bachelor pad must have looked like (minus the flat-screen TVs, of course). Larger rooms—the "Superior" ones and the suite—have old-fashioned bathtubs right in the bedroom, and all are done up with luxurious fabrics and beautiful prints of the London skyline. With all the amenities of a luxury hotel, but with infinitely more character, Fox and Anchor is pricey, but similar rooms can go for hundreds of pounds more in the City.

▶ ⚡ ⊖Barbican. Turn left onto Aldersgate St., left onto Charterhouse St,. then right onto Charterhouse Sq. *i* Book at least a few weeks in advance for the weekend. Free Wi-Fi. Ⓢ Deluxe rooms M-F £221, Sa-Su £137; Superior rooms £163-243; suite £243-327.

WESTMINSTER

🏰 Astor's Victoria   HOSTEL $
71 Belgrave Rd.
☎020 7834 3077

This branch of the Astor's family has all the chummy backpacker charm of the other locations, with the added benefit of recently refurbished rooms sporting new carpets and fresh paint. Even the larger dorms don't feel cramped, and those on the upper floors have wonderfully high ceilings. The staff goes out of their way to welcome guests, learning names and hosting pub crawls. Multiple common spaces give you the opportunity to make some friends of your own, too.

▶ ⚡ ⊖Victoria. Upon exiting the station, turn left onto Buckingham Palace Rd., and left onto Belgrave Rd. *i* Breakfast included. Female-only dorms available. Kitchen available until 10pm. Wi-Fi £1 per 40min., £5 per day. Ⓢ 4- to 8-bed dorms £14-23; doubles £25-35.

Victor Hotel   HOTEL $$$$
51 Belgrave Rd.
☎020 7592 9853; www.victorhotel.co.uk

It's no Mandarin Oriental, but, unlike many of the other townhouse hotels on Belgrave Rd., Victor has enough space for you and your suitcase to fit in the room at the same time. The rooms are basic, with limited decoration and simple furnishings, but they're clean, comfortable, and a good value for the area.

▶ ⚡ ⊖Victoria. Upon exiting the station, turn left onto Buckingham Palace Rd., and left onto Belgrave Rd. *i* Breakfast included. Free Wi-Fi. Ⓢ Singles £65-85; doubles £85-150; triples £110-160.

Accommodations

THE SOUTH BANK

👍 St. Christopher's Village HOSTEL $

165 Borough High St.

☎020 7939 9710; www.st-christophers.co.uk

This proud party hostel is the perfect place to make camp if you want convenient access to the city center as well as a more local, authentic neighborhood feel. The rooms are remarkably spacious—even the 22-bed dorm has its bunks lining the walls so there is plenty of open, glossy wood floor. St. Christopher's has all the amenities, including a chill-out room with a TV and DVDs to borrow, plus an action-packed bar next door. The hostel hosts karaoke, dance parties, and a 👍**Big Lebowski** night every Thursday, complete with £2 White Russians and a bowling excursion. If you're looking for a bit more peace and quiet, you can stay in the smaller St. Christopher's Inn next door or the female-only Oasis.

▶ ⇄ ⊖London Bridge. Walk down Borough High St. with the bridge at your back. *i* Breakfast included. Laundry and luggage storage included. Wi-Fi £2 per hr. [$] 4- to 22-bed dorms £12-23.

The Steam Engine HOSTEL $

41-42 Cosser St.

☎020 7928 0720; www.bestplaceinns.com

About as British as central London hostels get, the Steam Engine is perched on top of an old-fashioned pub, complete with faded pool table and garishly lit jukebox. Located down a small side street, the bar isn't particularly rowdy, and feels more like a rustic country establishment. The rooms upstairs have simple wooden bunks and not much else, though the beds certainly look comfortable. The downside is that the bunks have three beds, so perish the person who ends up sandwiched in the middle; the space is also probably not ideal for the very tall traveler. Guests get a variety of deals and after-hours access to the pub.

▶ ⇄ ⊖Lambeth North. Exit down Kennington Rd. and turn right onto Cosser St. *i* Breakfast included. Free Wi-Fi. [$] 9- and 12-bed dorms M-F £12-15, Sa-Su up to £27.

SOUTH KENSINGTON AND CHELSEA

This is not the place to come for budget accommodations. But while you can't walk a block without seeing a five-star luxury hotel, it is possible to find similar comfort at a much more affordable price.

Astor Hyde Park

HOSTEL $

191 Queen's Gate

☎020 7581 0103; www.astorhostels.co.uk

The flagship of the Astor Hostels chain, the Hyde Park location is all high ceilings, comfort, and aged grandeur—relics of its first life as a Victorian mansion. Rooms on the upper floors have massive French windows, and others feature domed glass skylights. The large common room, self-catering kitchen, and dining area make great hangout spaces. The endearing young staff organizes events like pub quizzes and beer Olympics every night.

► ⊖High St. Kensington. Turn right onto Kensington High St., then right onto Queen's Gate. *i* Breakfast included. Free Wi-Fi. Laundry available. [$] Dorms £15-26.

Smooth Criminal

London's long history has left behind some pretty absurd laws that never got taken off the books. Here are some you should probably know, as breaking them is very doable. Disclaimer: Let's Go does not endorse violating laws, even the stupid ones.

- **POSTAGE TREASON.** Don't put a stamp upside-down if it's got a picture of the Queen on it, or you might find yourself charged with treason against the crown.
- **CATTLE CALAMITY.** Sorry to break it to you, but you're going to have to wait until the evening to herd your cattle through Piccadilly Circus. One law stipulates that you cannot drive cattle down a road between the hours of 10am and 7pm, unless you've received authorization from the Police Commissioner.
- **ARMOR OFF.** Since 1313, it has been illegal to enter the House of Commons in a full suit of armor. (You have to wonder what incident led to that one being implemented.)
- **SOCKS ON.** Don't dare showcase your carefree spirit by walking barefoot past Buckingham Palace. It's illegal to be sockless within 100 yards of the monarch. We hope Prince Philip gets an exemption.

YHA London Holland Park
HOSTEL $

20 Holland Walk

☎020 7937 0748; www.yha.org.uk

A patchwork of three buildings (one of which is an old manor house), this is definitely not a typical hostel. The location at the rear of Holland Park makes it feel a bit like a park ranger's office. The tranquil garden, which features a fish-filled fountain and weird duck-like creatures, is particularly peaceful when there's a classical music concert in the park. The hostel is often crowded with school groups, but it still manages to be quieter than its competitors. The rooms are worn but well cleaned, with bunks stacked in Lego-like arrangements. The canteen serves breakfast and dinner, and there's also a kitchen available for guests' use.

▶ ⇞ ⊖High St. Kensington. Turn left onto Kensington High St., then right down Holland Walk in Holland Park. Look for signs for the hostel. ℹ Use night gate at the rear after 10pm when the park closes. All rooms are single sex. Laundry available. Wi-Fi £1 per 20min., £3 per hr., £5 per day, £9 per week. $ 12- to 20-bed dorms £15-23. ⏰ 7-day max. stay.

HYDE PARK TO NOTTING HILL

Given how swanky Notting Hill is, it's actually pretty surprising how many decently priced accommodations you can find here. Around Paddington are scores of simple hotels, but the ones farther south toward Hyde Park tend to offer more quality for comparable prices and convenience. Many of these establishments are tucked away on leafy residential streets, perfect for pretending that you're neighbors with some of the poshest people in London.

👍 Astor Quest
HOSTEL $

45 Queensborough Terr.

☎020 7229 7782; www.astorhostels.com

Astor Quest's rooms are par for the course in hostel-land, though the cherry-red metal bunks add a touch of mod flavor and the windows let in plenty of light and air. Breakfast is included and served in a room by the large kitchen, which is freely available for use (and has a seemingly unlimited supply of bread and peanut butter). You also have the unique experience of dining under Sid Vicious's drugged-out gaze. Be sure to ask the 24hr. reception for deals on clubs.

▶ ⇞ ⊖Bayswater. Take a right onto Queensway, left onto Bayswater Rd.,

then left onto Queensborough Terr. ℹ Ages 18-35 only. Luggage storage included. Laundry facilities available. Wi-Fi £5 per day. 1 female-only room available. [$] Dorms £14-23; twins £25-35.

Equity Point Hostel

HOSTEL $$

100-102 Westbourne Terr.

☎020 7087 8001; www.equity-point.com

It's always tempting to stumble out of the train station into the first hostel you see, but if that stumble happens to take you to this hostel's door, then you should consider yourself very lucky indeed. Rooms are decorated in blocks of bright color, with rainbow stripes stretching across the hallways, making the whole place feel cheerful. There's a common room with TV and video games, as well as a bar.

▶ ⊖Paddington. Make a right onto Praed St. and a right onto Westbourne Terr. ℹ Breakfast included. Wi-Fi available. [$] 4- to 8-bed dorms £20-34; doubles £92-113; triples £102-114.

The Pavilion

HOTEL $$$

34-36 Sussex Gardens

☎020 7262 0905; www.pavilionhoteluk.com

All you really need to know about the Pavilion is that the most popular room is named "Honky Tonk Afro." Besides blaxploitation, other rooms have themes ranging from Middle Eastern casbah to Baroque drawing room. The whole building feels like a drug-enhanced dream of a Victorian townhouse, with intensely colored velvet and stacks of oil paintings in ornate frames. This is definitely a standout among the rows of ordinary hotels lining the road.

▶ ⊖Paddington. Take a left onto Praed St., right onto London St., then a left onto Sussex Gardens. ℹ Continental breakfast included. [$] Small singles £60, large singles £85; doubles £100; triples £120; family rooms (quads) £130. 4% surcharge with credit card.

Hyde Park Hostel

HOSTEL $

2-6 Inverness Terr.

☎020 7727 9163; www.smartbackpackers.com

Right across from Hyde Park and surrounded by columned mansion entrances, this hostel will make you feel quite posh. Ten-bed dorms have high ceilings with intricate woodwork and lots of open space. While it doesn't seem to be a particularly convivial hostel, the price is excellent for the area.

▶ ⊖Bayswater. Take a right onto Queensway, left onto Bayswater, and then a left onto Inverness Terr. *i* 16+. Wi-Fi £1 per hr. Lockers £1.50 per day. Linens included. $ 4- to 14-bed dorms £10-16. ⏰ Reception 24hr. 2-week max. stay.

MARYLEBONE AND BLOOMSBURY

The northern part of this neighborhood, close to King's Cross, is packed with some of London's best hostels. Here, you can stay at a hostel where you can party all night without stepping outside your door, or somewhere that's more conducive to recovering from jet lag. Given the proximity to the station, there are also a number of nondescript hotels, though you're unlikely to find a good deal at any of them.

👍 Clink 78 — HOSTEL $

78 King's Cross Rd.

☎020 7183 9400; www.clinkhostels.com

The name of this hostel is not the only cheeky nod to the fact that the building it inhabits was once a courthouse and jail; its expertly renovated interior takes that theme and runs with it. Two common rooms on the main floor (one for internet access, one for TV and chilling out) are former courtrooms. Some of the private rooms are capsule-like "cells," set in what were once prisoners' quarters, and are definitely not for the claustrophobic. The dorms are brightly painted and covered in mod stencils, giving the rooms more character than those in most hostels. In the larger dorms, though, the bunks are packed together like they're in a prison. Downstairs is a self-catering kitchen, lots of picnic-like tables, and a popular bar that hosts events every night, from beer pong to karaoke to live DJs.

▶ ⊖King's Cross St. Paincras. Make a left from the station down Euston Rd. Follow it as it turns into Pentonville Rd., and then make a right onto King's Cross Rd. *i* Continental breakfast included. Luggage storage included. Laundry facilities available. Wi-Fi £1 per 30min., £5 per day, £15 per week. Female-only dorm available. $ 4- to 16-bed dorms £10-27; singles, doubles, and triples £40-90.

👍 Astors Museum Hostel — HOSTEL $

27 Montague St.

☎020 7580 5360; www.astorhostels.com

This is a true backpackers' hostel, quiet but centrally located (the name isn't kidding—it's directly across the street from the

British Museum). The staff live on-site and seem to have all the perks you could want at their fingertips: a good song on the reception speakers, an organized pub-crawl, a discount on local sights, and themed parties once per week. Astors is welcoming, comfortable, and exciting all at once. The rooms are spacious and simple, the kitchen is open for guest use, and everything is cleaned at least once daily.

▶ ⛙ ⊖Russell Sq. Go down Guilford toward Russell Sq., turn left into the square, and follow it around until you reach Montague St., then turn left. *i* Ages 18-35 only. Continental breakfast included. Luggage storage included. Laundry facilities available. Wi-Fi 40min. free upon arrival, £5 per day, £8 per week. Book 2 weeks in advance, 3 weeks for weekends. Female-only dorm available. $ 4- to 12-bed dorms £15-26; twins £60-80.

Generator Hostel HOSTEL $

37 Tavistock Pl.

☎020 7388 7666; www.generatorhostels.com

Upon waking up in the Generator Hostel after a night of revelry, you may wonder if you forgot to leave the club. To be fair, you don't even have to leave the building to indulge in debauchery—the downstairs bar is gigantic, has a DJ each night, and serves up every variation of Jagermeister you can think of. Theme parties are organized frequently (some with professional sponsors), and, with 900 beds, the hostel is a popular destination for bachelor and bachelorette parties. Actually want to get some sleep? The simple rooms lack the steel plates and neon lights of the common areas, but all have sinks and lockers. Massively popular and clearly well run, the hostel also has a canteen, travel shop, and cafe.

▶ ⛙ ⊖Russell Sq. Go down Colonnade away from Russell Sq. and turn left onto Grenville St.; follow it onto Hunter St. and turn left onto Tavistock Pl. *i* Breakfast included. Luggage storage included. Laundry available. Wi-Fi free for 1hr. Female-only dorms available. $ 4-to 12-bed dorms £15-30; singles £55-60. Other private rooms £20-30 per person. Check for frequent online deals. ⏰ Bar open 6pm-2am or later. Happy hour 6-9pm.

Clink 261 HOSTEL $

261-265 Gray's Inn Rd.

☎020 7833 9400; www.clinkhostels.com

The Clink 261 is the sister hostel of Clink 78, but with a more intimate, boutique-y feel and without a bar. If you dream of hostels where every night is movie night (where the film is picked by majority vote and watched from comfortable leather chairs), where cube chairs fill the entry, and where retro plastic coverings blanket every surface, then you've probably dreamed of Clink 261. Particularly notable is the large self-catering kitchen, with plenty of supplies and lots of room to hang out, though the beds themselves are packed together like sardines.

▶ # ⊖King's Cross St. Pancras. Turn left onto Euston Rd. and follow it as it curves right into Gray's Inn Rd. *i* Breakfast included. Luggage storage included. Laundry available. Wi-Fi £1 per 30min., £2 per 2hr. Female-only dorms available. $ Dorms £20-25; private rooms £50-75.

The George HOTEL $$$

58-60 Cartwright Gardens

☎020 7387 8777; www.georgehotel.com

The rooms at The George are grandiose in space and furnishings, with a somewhat more inspired decorating scheme (interesting prints on the walls and luxurious bedspreads) than most inexpensive hotels. Tucked away from the main streets of busy Bloomsbury, the George is a quiet and cozy hotel that'll let you sleep, without keeping you too far from the action.

▶ # ⊖Russell Sq. Go down Colonnade away from Russell Sq. and turn left onto Grenville St., follow it onto Hunter St., and turn left onto Cartwright Gardens. *i* Full English breakfast included. Free Wi-Fi. $ Singles £59, with bath £79; doubles £79/97; triples £95/115; quads with bath £109. Discounts for stays longer than 5 nights.

NORTH LONDON

👍 Palmer's Lodge Swiss Cottage HOSTEL $

40 College Crescent

☎020 7483 8470; www.palmerslodge.co.uk

Northwest London may feel like a random place to stay, but this location provides easy access to Hampstead Heath, and public transportation will bring you to the center of town in 10min. What's more, the hostel is consistently one of the highest-rated in London. It's easy to see why: dorms are spacious and feature linen curtains and carved wooden bunks reminiscent of a treehouse. The common spaces are plentiful and comfortable, and the staff is tremendously accommodating. Palmer's Lounge is located in a giant refurbished Victorian house that feels like the school in *X-Men,* except there are backpackers instead of mutants. The bar, with its enclosed terrace and squishy armchairs, is particularly inviting. All the dorms are single-sex.

▶ ⊖Swiss Cottage. Take exit 2 from the station, turn left onto Eton Ave., then right onto College Crescent. ℹ Breakfast included. 18+. Free Wi-Fi. [$] Dorms £16-30; doubles from £35.

St. Christopher's Camden — HOSTEL $

50 Camden High St.

☎020 7388 1012; www.st-christophers.co.uk

This outpost of the St. Christopher's hostel chain puts you in the heart of Camden Town, and all the good and bad that entails. The rooms may feel a touch boring (just metal bunks with little other decoration), but each dorm includes an ensuite bathroom. Downstairs is the usual attached pub, with ample drinks and meal specials.

▶ ⊖Camden Town. Turn left onto Camden High St. (walking away from the market). ℹ Breakfast included. Free Wi-Fi. [$] Dorms £17-28.

EAST LONDON

👍 The Hoxton — HOTEL $$$

81 Great Eastern St.

☎020 7550 1000; www.hoxtonhotels.com

The Hoxton is a large, elegant hotel that would break the bank if it weren't for their incredible pricing structure. Every room is the same, so there's no confusion about what a "super-deluxe-luxury-magical-suite" entails, and each goes for the same price on a given day. If you book well in advance, you can save up to two-thirds off the price—plus, unlike many London establishments, their rates tend to go down on the weekends. Best of all: four times per year they have a sale where 500 rooms are sold for just £1. The rooms themselves are fantastic: great views, fluffy beds, sleek furniture, and plenty of amenities.

▶ ⊖Old St. Veer right at the roundabout, go down Old St., and then turn right onto Great Eastern St. ℹ Breakfast included. 1hr. of free international landline calls per day. Free Wi-Fi. [$] Rooms £59-199, depending on when you book.

Queen Mary University Campus Accommodations — DORM $$

Mile End Rd.

☎020 7882 8177; www.accommodation.qmul.ac.uk

This East London university opens its dorms to travelers

during the summer, roughly from mid-June to mid-September. The rooms are arranged in six- to nine-person flats, and each room has access to a kitchen and living room. You can relive your college days in these simple rooms, with twin beds, standard wardrobes, and desks. The dorms are arranged in a "student village" with laundromat, restaurants, and a convenience store. For long stays, this is one of the best options in London. The location may seem a bit out of the way, but a short walk to the Tube station means you can be in the city center within 20min.

▶ ⚡ ⊖Mile End. Turn left down Mile End Rd. The campus will be across the canal, on your right. The accommodations office is at point 4 on the campus map, on the main road. *i* Breakfast included with B and B prices. Flats cleaned weekly during longer stays. Ⓢ B and B singles £42-49; twins £60-65. Weekly singles £154, with bath £175; additional night £25. Credit card only.

SOUTH LONDON

Journeys London Bridge Hostel   HOSTEL $
204 Manor Pl.
☎020 7735 6581; www.visitjourneys.com

Pretty much the only budget accommodation in South London, this hostel is located in a fairly quiet area just a short distance from the Tube. Journeys has all of the usual hostel amenities, including a bar, common room, and kitchen. The nine- and 12-bed dorms all have three-bed bunks, but each comes with its own curtain and reading lamp. The rooms may feel a bit dark thanks to the subdued color scheme of the carpets and walls.

▶ ⚡ ⊖Kennington. Make a left onto Braganza St. and then a left onto Manor Pl. *i* Breakfast included. Free Wi-Fi. Female-only dorms available. Ⓢ Dorms £10-18.

WEST LONDON

The Monkeys in the Trees   HOSTEL $
49 Becklow Rd.
☎020 8749 9197; www.monkeysinthetrees.co.uk

The Monkeys in the Trees may be a bit far from the city center, but immersing yourself in this residential neighborhood will give you a real feel for the city. Bright, cheery dorms are located above a classic pub. Guests have access to the bar and its garden as well as a TV lounge with movies and board games, plus a kitchen. The three-bed bunks are a bit of a squeeze, but each bed has its own curtain and reading light for a bit of privacy.

▸ ⊖Shepherd's Bush Market. Cross Uxbridge Rd. and make a right, then a left onto Becklow Rd. It's about a 15min. walk. Alternatively, take bus #207 or 260 to Wormholt Rd. *i* Breakfast included. Luggage storage included. Free Wi-Fi. [$] Dorms £13-20.

St. Christopher's Hammersmith HOSTEL $

28 Hammersmith Broadway

☎020 8748 5285; www.st-christophers.co.uk

St. Christopher's is truly on top of the action—the hostel sits over its own busy bar (where guests receive a 10% discount), which is itself right on top of the Hammersmith Tube station. The rooms retain many of the details of the venerable old building, like wooden floors, fireplaces, and elegant windows. The bathrooms, fortunately, are entirely modern. The staff here are always ready to organize events or give tips for a good night out.

▸ ⊖Hammersmith. It's right above the Tube entrance on Hammersmith Broadway. *i* Breakfast included. Wi-Fi £2 per hr. Female-only dorms available. [$] Dorms £15-25.

Sights

From the time Londinium was a rainy outpost of ancient Rome to the days when it governed a quarter of the world, London has accumulated a few worthwhile sights. A little religion called Christianity came along and led to the elegant churches of Christopher Wren. Centuries of exploration around the world deposited a bounty of treasures into the British Museum. The monarchy's predilection for home improvement scattered palaces across the city. A thriving 20th-century art scene produced some of the best (and strangest) modern art you'll ever see. Don't worry—all this splendor is accessible to travelers on a budget, as most of the city's major museums are free. Trying to see a church? Look for service times, as you can frequently get in free by attending Eucharist or Evensong. Even if you can't afford to visit all of the sights individually, save up to buy a ticket to St. Paul's Golden Gallery—the view from the top is worth every penny.

Don't limit your experience to ticketed sights, either. London's history is everywhere. Whatever path you choose—whether you're strolling down the winding streets of Marylebone or stalking the curry houses of Brick Ln.—your exploration will be rewarded. There's no wrong turn. Unless you're on the Hampstead Heath and you hear a strange growling to your left. In that case, a left turn may be the wrong one.

Budget Sights

Though London is a pricey city overall, sights are one thing that you won't have to shell out for. Call it nice, maybe call it dumb, but the Brits have conveniently made most of their big-name historic sights free to the public. Walk around a free world-class museum. Take a jaunt around Hyde Park. Sneak into Evensong to see one of the many churches. London is a spectacle in and of itself. Open your eyes, close your wallet, and let London entertain you.

THE CITY OF LONDON

Many of London's most popular sights are found here, and they shouldn't be missed—even if you'll be surrounded by camera-dependent tourists with the same idea.

🖾 Saint Paul's Cathedral CHURCH

St. Paul's Churchyard
☎020 7246 8350; www.stpauls.co.uk

It's something of a challenge to enter St. Paul's Cathedral and not take the Lord's name in vain. The church is epically grandiose, whether it's the huge size, ornate ceilings, or glowing stained glass that attract your eyes. This is the fourth cathedral to stand on this site, the first dating back to 604 CE. The third incarnation was destroyed, like so much of London, in the Great Fire of 1666. Architect Christopher Wren rebuilt many of London's churches after the fire, but St. Paul's, consecrated in 1708, is his masterpiece. From the start, Wren fought to include the fantastic dome that is now visible throughout the city, but the Church of England was hesitant to include an architectural feature that was so characteristically Roman Catholic. Ultimately, Wren won. If you're able to pull your eyes away from the dome—one of the highest in the world—look out for the cathedral's other highlights: the terrifyingly huge memorial to the **Duke of Wellington** (on your left in the north aisle as you walk through the nave); William Holman Hunt's *The Light of the World* in the Middlesex Chapel (which is set aside for private prayer); Henry Moore's strikingly modern *Mother and Child* sculpture, and the memorial to American and British servicemen in WWII.

We know what you're really thinking, and, yes, you are allowed to climb to the top of the **dome.** After 257 dizzyingly

Something Old, Something Blue

If you see a little blue plaque out of the corner of your eye, stop! These little signs mark the sites where famous Londoners have lived. Here are a few highlights:

If you wander the streets around Marylebone, you may come across one of the newest plaques at 34 Montague Sq. Though the plaque is dedicated to John Lennon and Yoko Ono, who had their first London home here, the property was originally bought by Ringo Starr and rented to both Paul McCartney and—sorry, George—Jimi Hendrix.

A short distance away, you can find Hendrix's other London home at 23 Brook St., which is physically connected to George Frederick Handel's place at number 25. Though Lennon's home is not open to the public, both Hendrix's and Handel's abodes have been combined to host the Handel House Museum. (☎020 7495 1685 ⇄ Oxford Circus. $ £6, concessions £5, under 17 £2. ⏰ Open Tu-W 10am-6pm, Th 10am-8pm, F-Sa 10am-6pm, Su noon-6pm.)

If you're around Bloomsbury, don't miss the plaque dedicated to Charles Dickens at 48 Doughty St. You can even go inside and see his original manuscripts. (☎020 7405 2127 ⇄ Russell Sq. or Farringdon. $ £7, concessions £5, under 10 free. ⏰ Open daily 10am-5pm.)

tight wooden steps, visitors find themselves in the **Whispering Gallery,** a seating area around the inner ring of the dome where, under the right conditions, you can hear a whisper from the other side. Many people try this simultaneously, which makes standing at the rim of the dome feel a bit like one of the scarier whisper segments in *Lost,* but it's worth giving this acoustic novelty a try. The climb is greatly enhanced if you make the journey while a choir sings in the nave; the acoustics in the Whispering Gallery are incredible. After 376 steps, visitors can climb out onto the **Stone Gallery,** which is open-air, low-stress, and thoroughly enjoyable. Then it's another 152 steps to the **Golden Gallery,** which offers an incredible view over the city. During WWII, the army used this gallery to spot German planes up to 10 miles away. Once you've been to the top, descend beneath the cathedral to find a veritable who's who of famous Britons—including Horatio Nelson, Florence Nightingale, the Duke of Wellington, William Blake, Henry

Moore, and Christopher Wren—buried in St. Paul's **crypt.** Wren's inconspicuous tomb (to the right of the OBE Chapel) is inscribed *"Lector, si monumentum requiris circumspice,"* meaning, "Reader, if you seek his monument, look around."

▸ ⊖St. Paul's. Signs outside the station lead you to the cathedral. *i* 1½hr. free guided tours at 10:45, 11:15am, 1:30, and 2pm. Briefer introductory tours run throughout the day. A handheld multimedia tour is included in the price of admission. $ £14.50, concessions £13.50, children £5.50. ⏰ Open M-Sa 8:30am-4pm. You can get in for free (though you'll have limited access) during church services. Matins M-Sa 7:30am. Eucharist M-Sa 8am and 12:30pm; Su 8, 11am, and 6pm. Evensong M-Sa 5pm, Su 3:15pm. Free organ recitals Su 4:45-5:15pm. Service times subject to change; check the website or the signs outside the cathedral.

👍 The Temple

HISTORICAL SITE

Between Essex St. and Temple Ave.

☎020 7427 4820

The Temple is a stunning complex of medieval, Elizabethan, and Victorian buildings, first established by the Knights Templar in 1185 as the English seat for the order (and catapulted into stardom by *The Da Vinci Code*). After the Knights were disbanded at the beginning of the 14th century, the buildings were leased to lawyers, and the site is now devoted to two of London's Inns of Court, legal and parliamentary offices, and training grounds for baby lawyers. The gardens, medieval church, and Middle Temple Hall are occasionally open to the public. Middle Temple Hall (www.middletemple.org.uk) is an excellent example of Elizabethan architecture with its beautiful double hammer beam roof. Originally used as a stable, it is now famous for hosting the premiere of Shakespeare's 👍**Twelfth Night** in 1602. The large gardens are perfectly manicured with lush shrubberies and provide a handy spot for quiet reflection. The church (www.templechurch.com) has phenomenal stained glass windows and a grand vaulted ceiling. Opening hours for the various sites are erratic, but even when things are closed, the labyrinthine paths around the Temple's many buildings are well worth the visit.

▸ ⊖Temple. Go to the Victoria Embankment, turn left, and turn left again at Temple Ln. *i* Book 1hr. tours in advance. You can book to stay for lunch if you're appropriately dressed. $ Church and tours free. ⏰ Middle Temple Hall open M-F 10am-noon and 3-4pm, except when in use. Hours for church vary, but are posted outside. Services Oct-July Su 11:15am. Organ recitals Oct-July W 1:15-1:45pm. Tours Oct-July Tu-F 11am.

👍 Museum of London
MUSEUM

150 London Wall

☎020 7001 9844; www.museumoflondon.org.uk

The Museum of London is an exhaustive celebration of the city, tracing its history from the pre-Roman days to the present through timelines, reconstructions, and artifacts. The fascinating pieces of history on display include a replica of a London Saxon house from the mid-11th century, a beautiful model of the original St. Paul's Cathedral, a taxi from 1908, and Beatlemania paraphernalia. Relatively compact for its scope, the Museum of London gives you a sense for the city's development and how it grew into the international metropolis that you see today.

▶ ⇄ ⊖St. Paul's. Go up St. Martins and Aldersgate. $ Free. ⏰ Open M-F 10am-6pm. 45min. tours at 11am, noon, 3, and 4pm.

👍 Courtauld Gallery
MUSEUM

Somerset House, Strand

☎020 7872 0220; www.courtauld.ac.uk

Courtauld Gallery is a very small gallery in a very large house. The famous 👍**KGB** double agent, Anthony Blunt, was director of this gallery for nearly 30 years. The collection includes medieval and Renaissance art from the likes of Botticelli and Rubens, but it's most renowned for its delightful Impressionist and post-Impressionist collection, featuring paintings by Degas, Monet, Manet (including 👍**A Bar at the Folies-Bergère**), Seurat, and van Gogh. Upstairs, you'll find works by Cezanne, Pissarro, Matisse, and Kandinsky.

▶ ⇄ ⊖Temple. Turn right onto Temple Pl., left onto Arundel St., then left onto Strand. $ £6, concessions £4.50. Free on M 10am-2pm. ⏰ Open daily 10am-6pm.

Tower Bridge
BRIDGE

☎020 7403 3761; www.towerbridge.org.uk

Erected between 1886 and 1894, Tower Bridge was built when London Bridge became too crowded—and, perhaps, as a little insurance in case the bridge they'd been singing about really did fall down. Unlike London Bridge, Tower Bridge does not disappoint on the aesthetic front. It's a bascule bridge, meaning that you might get to see it rise—check the bridge lift times online if you don't want to leave it to chance. The exhibition you can pay to get into is enjoyable, but might not be for those afraid of heights. Hear fun facts and enchanting anecdotes, like the story of a 1952 double-decker bus that accidentally jumped the bridge while it was rising—clearly the driver never heard the phrase "mind the gap." Tower Bridge is less of a tourist trap than the Tower of London, though you can skip the ticket price and just enjoy its stunning architecture for free.

▶ ⚲ ⊖ Tower Hill. Follow signs to Tower Bridge. Ⓢ £8, concessions £5.60, ages 5-15 £3.40, under 5 free. ⏰ Open daily Apr-Sept 10am-6:30pm; Oct-Mar 9:30am-6pm. Last entry 1hr. before close.

Tower of London   HISTORICAL SITE

Between Tower Hill and the Thames
☎0844 482 7777; www.hrp.org.uk/toweroflondon

In its 1000-year history, the Tower of London has been a fortress, a royal palace, a prison, a zoo, a mint, the site of the first royal observatory, and, now, a tourist trap. If tourists were an invading army in the days of William the Conqueror, he would have surrendered instantly. Unusually dressed men and women, known as "Beefeaters," guard and live in the tower as well as give guided tours. Despite its name, there are actually multiple towers in the complex, each with its own myths and anecdotes. **Wakefield Tower** is near the home of six famous ravens—legend claims that if they fly away the white tower will crumble and disaster will befall the monarchy. The **Bloody Tower,** built in 1225, is allegedly where Richard III had the young King Edward V and his brother Richard ("The Princes in the Tower") murdered—what is thought to be their remains were found under a staircase two centuries later. The **White Tower,** built by William the Conqueror in 1078, is the oldest part of the Tower. It was once a royal palace: the top floor was reserved for kings and queens, the floor below housed the servants, and the basement served as a dungeon (and guest house!). The **Jewel House** boasts gemstones with enough glitter to induce a seizure, and it contains the royal family's famous **Crown Jewels.** The jewels are the focal point of many people's visits to the tower, so arrive as early as possible. Inside, you'll see the sovereign's scepter highlighted by a cross featuring the **First Star of Africa** (the largest perfect diamond in the world at 530.2 carats). Outside the Tower lies **Tower Hill,** the execution site where Anne Boleyn lost her head; her ghost is said to haunt the chapel of **St. Peter ad Vincula** (the Tower's chapel), where she's also buried. The last executions to take place here were of prisoners convicted of espionage during WWII.

Sights

▶ � ⊖Tower Hill. *i* Buy tickets at the Tube station or at the Welcome Center, as these places tend to be less crowded. Ⓢ £19.80, concessions £17.05, under 5 free. Audio tours £4, students £3. Ⓩ Open Mar-Oct M 10am-5:30pm, Tu-Sa 9am-5:30pm, Su 10am-5:30pm; Nov-Feb M 10am-4:30pm, Tu-Sa 9am-5:30pm, Su 10am-4:30pm. Last entry Mar-Oct 5pm; Nov-Feb 4:30pm.

St Stephen Walbrook   CHURCH

39 Walbrook

☎020 7626 9000; www.ststephenwalbrook.net

The marshmallow-like object sitting in the center of the room is actually Henry Moore's controversial idea of what an altar should look like. Rumored to have "the most perfectly proportioned interior in the world," St Stephen Walbrook, a Saxon church built in the seventh century, is yet another beautiful Christopher Wren construction. It's unusually square, with pews arranged in a circle around the aforementioned altar. Offsetting the white walls and large, arched windows is a magnificently carved dark wood pulpit. The church used to be bordered by a river, and the structure slips downward in a continuous battle against gravity. Visit toward the end of a summer day to bask in the light that floods through the glass windows.

▶ � ⊖Mansion House. Turn right onto Cannon St., then left onto Walbrook. Ⓢ Free. Ⓩ Open M-F 10am-4pm. Organ recitals F 12:30pm. Eucharist M 1pm.

Clockmakers' Museum   MUSEUM

Inside Guildhall Library off Aldermanbury

☎020 7332 1868

The Clockmakers' Museum is sort of like the interior of Doc Brown's house from *Back to the Future,* except with more clocks. Each clock, watch, sundial, and chronometer from the 500-year history of clocks is explained in this one-room museum. For those less inclined to horological technology, the museum has famous watches and clocks, including some of the first mass-produced watches and the watch worn by Sir Edmund Hillary during his 1953 climb of Mount Everest. The museum is worth a brief visit, if only to hear the sound of so many clocks ticking in unison.

▶ � ⊖St. Paul's. Go down Cheapside with your back to St. Paul's Cathedral. Turn left onto King St., left onto Gresham, and right onto Aldermanbury. Enter through the library. Ⓢ Free. Ⓩ Open M-Sa 9:30am-4:45pm.

THE WEST END

Thanks to the street performers around Convent Garden, enough theaters to make drama-school kids think acting is a promising career, and a generally bustling atmosphere, the West End is something of a sight in itself. The area around **Trafalgar Square** is home to some of the city's most interesting museums and monuments.

National Gallery — MUSEUM

Trafalgar Sq.

☎020 7747 2885; www.nationalgallery.org.uk

The National Gallery presides over Trafalgar Sq. and is perhaps even more impressive than the square itself. Founded in 1824 and moved to its current location in 1838, the gallery encompasses all the major traditions of Western European art from the Middle Ages (housed in the **Sainsbury Wing**) to the early 20th century. Works are arranged chronologically and then geographically, so if you're fascinated by 16th-century Dutch painting, you can make a beeline for Room Five. Some rooms are packed floor to ceiling with Italian masterpieces by Michelangelo and Raphael; if you really want to piss people off, ask them where they're keeping the Donatellos. We have to put in a plug for Room 30, a must-see for any aspiring mustache-growers: see Velázquez's 1656 *Philip IV of Spain* for curl, and Juan Bautista del Mazo's *Don Adrián Pulido Pareja* for volume and under-lip work. When all of the stern portraits, religious iconography, and pastoral allegories get to be too much, move on to the gallery of 18th- to early 20th-century paintings. Here you'll find a number of British artists, including Turner, plus plenty of works by Frenchmen like Manet, Monet, and Cézanne. Many people think that the best way to view an Impressionist work is to squint and back away from it. We share this not to advise you, but rather to explain why people keep crashing into you. If knowing where you are is important to you, don't forget to pick up a map at the entrance (£1)—the museum is just one floor, but it's one huge floor.

▶ ⇄ ⊖Charing Cross. $ Free. Special exhibits around £10. Audio tours £3.50, students £2.50. ⏰ Open M-Th 10am-6pm, F 10am-9pm, Sa-Su 10am-6pm. 1hr. guided tours daily at 11:30am and 2:30pm; meet at Sainsbury Wing info desk. Additional tour F at 7pm. 10min. talks on individual paintings M-Tu 4pm, F-Su 4pm.

National Portrait Gallery — MUSEUM

St. Martin's Pl.

☎020 7306 0055; www.npg.org.uk

In London, it's easy to get lost in history. You have to remember names of monarchs, gossip stars, the insanely wealthy, the star-crossed lovers—and we haven't even talked about those outside of the royal family. The National Portrait Gallery is less about the art than it is about the subjects of the portraits and what they meant for England. The gallery presents excellent short histories of the individuals and organizes the rooms to trace British history through its greatest assets: its women and men. It also answers the all-consuming question: which of your favorite British royals, politicians, writers, and scientists were total hotties? There are loads of kings, queens, and plenty of Churchill and other Prime Ministers in the imposing **Statesmen's Gallery,** but there are also rooms devoted to thinkers and popular figures. You can see poets Byron (hottie) and Andrew Marvell (nottie—no wonder he resorted to poetry for seduction); scientists like Charles Darwin and Michael Faraday (no, not the dude from *Lost*); and novelists like Jane Austen and James Joyce. As you get to the contemporary portraits, things get a little bit more experimental and the faces can be less easy to identify. These modern portraits include Marc Quinn's *Self,* much of which is made from the artist's frozen blood (talk about suffering for your art). For the less squeamish, there are photographs of fan favorites like Princes William and Harry, George Michael, and Iman. Each summer, the gallery hosts selections from the BP Portrait Award contest, showing the best international portraits of the past year.

► 🚆 ⊖Charing Cross. Walk down Strand to Trafalgar Sq. and turn right. $ Free. Small special exhibits £5, large exhibitions £10. Audio tours £3. ⏰ Open M-W 10am-6pm, Th-F 10am-9pm, Sa-Su 10am-6pm. Guided tours Tu 3pm, Th 1:15pm, Sa-Su 3pm. Open until 10pm on select nights; check website for details.

Trafalgar Square — HISTORICAL SITE

Trafalgar Sq. is one of the many places in central London where oodles of people are packed amid gorgeous architecture. This is arguably the most famous of all those places, and it has some of the best architecture and seemingly almost all of the people. Designed by Sir Charles Barry, who also designed the Houses of Parliament, Trafalgar Sq.

Sights

commemorates **Admiral Horatio Nelson.** The **National Gallery** stands to the north of the square, and the rest is lined with grand buildings belonging to various international institutions. The central space serves as a meeting point, demonstration area, and the home of an annual Christmas tree (donated by Norway in thanks for service given in WWII). A sandstone statue of Nelson tops the square's most notable feature: the 50m tall **Nelson's Column.** It's a pretty impressive sight, especially against the backdrop of **St Martin-in-the-Fields's** spires at the edge of the plaza. The four panels at the column's base celebrate Nelson's naval victories at St. Vincent (1797), the Nile (1798), Copenhagen (1801), and Trafalgar (1805). A bronze lion rests on each corner of the block supporting the column—children climb all over them and occasionally dangle from their mouths. There are two beautiful fountains in the square, each with teal statues of strange merpeople holding fish. Perhaps even more jarring, the water is an unnatural shade of aquamarine—so blue that it makes the Thames look black, instead of just sickly green.

▶ 🚉 ⊖Charing Cross.

St Martin-in-the-Fields — CHURCH

Trafalgar Sq.

☎020 7766 1100; www.smitf.org

In the 16th century, Henry VIII significantly renovated the medieval version of this church to keep plague victims away from his palace. The building's current incarnation is a Neoclassical marvel, with a large columned terrace and a beautifully carved arched ceiling. The architecture was originally panned, but it went on to inspire the design of many early American churches. St Martin's is the parish church of the royal family, but it's best known for its strong musical tradition. Every Monday, Tuesday, and Friday at 1pm, the church holds a 45min. "lunchtime concert," a classical recital from students at musical academies and colleges. In the evening, more renowned artists perform in the beautiful space.

▶ 🚉 ⊖Charing Cross. It's on the eastside of Trafalgar Sq. ℹ Jazz concerts W 8pm. $ Free. Lunchtime concerts £3.50 suggested donation. Reserved ticket for jazz £9, unreserved £5.50. ⏰ Open M-Tu 8:30am-1pm and 2-6pm, W 8:30am-1:15pm and 2-5pm, Th 8:30am-1:15pm and 2-6pm, F 8:30am-1pm and 2-6pm, Sa 9:30am-6pm, Su 3:30-5pm. Open at other times for services and concerts.

Sights

WESTMINSTER

[✓] Westminster Abbey
CHURCH, HISTORICAL SITE

Off Parliament Sq.

☎020 7222 5152; www.westminster-abbey.org

London has no shortage of lovely churches steeped in history. But Westminster Abbey stands out as the best combination of historical importance, breathtaking beauty, and a still-vibrant community of worshippers. The kernel (the Romanesque-style center of the church) was built in the mid-11th century by Edward the Confessor. You can trace the development of English architecture through the later additions, from the Gothic nave (the highest in England) to the Lady Chapel, built in the Late English Gothic style, with a ceiling that looks like carved lace. While the vaulted ceilings and glowing stained glass might tempt you to keep your neck craned upward, don't miss the exquisite Cosmati pavement in front of the altar. At its center is the spot where every English sovereign since William the Conqueror has been crowned.

While the Abbey is undeniably a tourist attraction (and an expensive one at that), it is still, first and foremost, a functioning house of worship. Nearly all important British church ceremonies take place here, including last year's royal wedding. Pilgrims come here from across the world, and its daily services are packed with people taking in the atmosphere of a place that's been the scene of prayer for over 1000 years. We recommend visiting for Evensong—not only is it free and less crowded, but seeing the Abbey in action with the sound of the choir is an experience you won't soon forget.

▶ 🚉 ⊖Westminster. Walk away from the river. Parliament Sq. and the Abbey will be on your left. *i* The Abbey vergers offer 1½hr. tours. $ £16, students and seniors £13, ages 11-18 £6, under 11 free. Verger-led tours £3. ⏰ Open M-Tu 9:30am-3:30pm, W 9:30am-6pm, Th-Sa 9:30am-3:30pm. Verger-led tours M-F 10, 10:30, 11am, 2 and 2:30pm; Sa 10, 10:30, and 11am. Services: M-F Matins 7:30am, Holy Communion 8am and 12:30pm, choral Evensong 5pm (spoken on W); Sa 8am Morning Prayer, 9am Holy Communion, 3pm choral Evensong (June-Sept 5pm); Su 8am Holy Communion, 10am Choral Matins, 11:15am Sung Eucharist, 3pm Choral Evensong, 5:45pm organ recital, 6:30pm Evening Prayer.

🏛 Churchill Museum and Cabinet War Rooms
MUSEUM, HISTORICAL SITE

Clive Steps, King Charles St.
☎020 7930 6961; www.iwm.org.uk/cabinet

The Cabinet War Rooms opened in 1939, just a few days before the outbreak of WWII. They were used as a shelter for important government officers, and Winston Churchill spent almost every day of the war in the windowless, airless subterranean rooms, recreated vividly in this museum. The rooms are tense with wartime anxiety, and the map room, with lights that were never turned off during the war's six years, still burn brightly. Connected to the Cabinet War Rooms is the Churchill Museum. Visitors can step on sensors to hear excerpts from some of his most famous speeches and watch videos detailing the highs and lows of his career. Also on display are his alcohol habits, which included drinks with every meal, and his signature "romper," better known as a onesie. The interactive, touchscreen "lifeline" is phenomenally detailed; be sure to touch his 90th birthday and August 6th, 1945, but be prepared to draw stares from the other museum patrons. It should be noted that, while a lock of Churchill's hair is on display, the heavy security surrounding it makes it impossible to use a voodoo doll or potion to bring the great man back to life.

▶ ⚑ ⊖Westminster. Turn right down Parliament St., and left onto King Charles St. Ⓢ £16, students and seniors £13, disabled £8, under 16 free. ⓠ Open daily 9:30am-6pm. Last entry 5pm.

Houses of Parliament
HISTORICAL SITE

Westminster Palace
www.parliament.uk

The iconic Palace of Westminster is the home of the United Kingdom's two houses of Parliament: the House of Lords and the House of Commons. This super-pointy Gothic structure was built in the mid-19th century, after a fire consumed the earlier complex of buildings that stood on this spot (more recent renovations repaired bomb damage from the Blitz). It's hard to do justice to the sheer majesty of this complex of three towers, 1000 rooms, and three miles of corridor. For the best view of the entire structure, head to the south bank of the Thames—especially at dusk, when the palace is lit up. Besides holding the chambers where the two Houses hold their debates, the Palace is the location of countless Parliamentary offices, committee chambers, and rooms for ceremonial functions (notably Westminster Hall, a relic from the 11th century). The Houses are steeped in countless rumors, stories, and strange practices. Some of our favorites include the tradition that the Yeomen of the Guard check the basement of the Palace whenever Parliament opens (ever since Guy Fawkes's Gunpowder Plot of 1605), and that, though eating and drinking are prohibited in the Commons, the Chancellor of the Exchequer may have an alcoholic drink in hand when giving the budget speech (Disraeli went with brandy and water, while Gladstone preferred sherry with a beaten egg).

There are a number of ways members of the public can visit the Houses of Parliament. Debates in both Houses are generally open to the public; visitors can queue for admission during sitting times, though entrance is not guaranteed. Nor is it guaranteed that anything interesting will be going on—we recommend checking the website to see what bills are on the table. Question Times are livelier, though tickets may only be reserved by UK residents, so foreign visitors can only take the rare leftover spaces. Visitors can also watch committee meetings on more specific topics, like Science and Technology or Foreign Affairs; the weekly schedule of these sessions is posted on the website as well. Finally, tours of the Houses are given throughout the year, but foreign visitors can only attend on Saturdays and during the Summer Recess (August and September).

▸ ‡ ⊖Westminster. The public entrance is at Cromwell Green, on St. Margaret St., directly across from Westminster Abbey. $ Debates and committee

For Ben the Bell Tolls

Everybody knows about London's signature timekeeper, Big Ben. But while most people use the name to refer to the 316 ft. tall monster clock tower above the Palace of Westminster, it actually belongs to the huge bell inside of it. The most common theory about the name is that the bell was named for Sir Benjamin Hall, a civil engineer who oversaw the final reconstruction of the Houses of Parliament. Calling our friend Ben merely "big" is like suggesting that the Hulk could get a little cheesed off: the bell has a width of 8 ft. and clocks in at around 13.5 tons. We guess "Humongous Ben" just wouldn't have the same catchy alliteration.

sessions free. Tours £15, concessions £10, children £6. ☎ When Parliament is in session, House of Commons open M-Tu 2:30-10:30pm, W 11:30am-7:30pm, Th 10:30am-6:30pm, sometimes F 9:30am-3pm; House of Lords open M-Tu 2:30-10pm, W 3-10pm, Th 11am-7:30pm, sometimes F 10am-close of business. Tours leave every 15min. Aug M-Tu 9:15am-4:30pm, W 1:15-4:30pm, Th 9:15-4:30pm; Sept M 9:15am-4:30pm, Tu-Th 1:15-4:30pm, F-Sa 9:15am-4:30pm; Oct-July Sa 9:15am-4:30pm.

Buckingham Palace

PALACE, HISTORICAL SITE

The Mall

☎020 7766 7300; www.royalcollection.org.uk

Cushy though it is, Buckingham Palace wasn't originally built for the royals. George III bought it from the Duke of Buckingham which in 1761 for his wife, Queen Charlotte, who gave birth to 14 out of her 15 children here. The house was expanded by their son, George IV (the one who wasn't born here), who commissioned John Nash to transform the existing building into a palace. In 1837, Queen Victoria moved in, and it has remained a royal residence ever since.

The **Changing of the Guard** takes place here every day at 11:30am from April to late July, and then on alternate days throughout the rest of the year. Forget the dumb American movies where obnoxious tourists try to make the unflinching guards move; they are far enough away that tourists can do no more than whistle every time they move three feet and salute. The entire spectacle lasts 40min.; to see it, you should show up well before 11:30am and stand in front of the palace in view of the morning guards. The middle of the week is the least crowded time to watch.

The interior of the palace is, for the most part, closed to the public—we can't imagine the Queen would be pleased with tourists tramping through her tearoom. From late July to early October, though, the royals head to Scotland and the **State Rooms** are opened to the public. These rooms are used for formal occasions, so they're as sumptuous and royal as you could hope they'd be. They feature fine porcelain, furniture, paintings, and sculptures by famous artists like Rembrandt and Rubens. In addition to the permanent pieces, the rooms often exhibit treasures from the Royal Collection—jewels, Fabergé eggs, and Kate Middleton's wedding dress. The **Royal Mews,** open most of the year, functions as a museum, stable, riding school, and a working carriage house. The carriages are fantastic—especially the "Glass Coach," which carries royal brides to their weddings, and the four-ton Gold State Coach. Unfortunately, the magic pumpkin carriage used to escape from evil step-royals is only visible until midnight, but if you're in the Royal Mews past midnight, you have other problems. Finally, the **Queen's Gallery** is dedicated to temporary exhibitions of jaw-droppingly valuable items from the Royal Collection. Five rooms designed to look like the interior of the palace are filled with glorious artifacts that the Queen holds in trust for the nation. They feature everything from Dutch landscape paintings to photographs of Antarctic expeditions to Leonardo da Vinci's anatomical drawings.

▶ 🚆 ⊖Victoria. Turn right onto Buckingham Palace Rd. and follow it to Buckingham Gate. ℹ Audio tour provided for State Rooms. $ State Rooms £18, students and seniors £16.50, ages 5-16 £10.25, under 5 free. Royal Mews £8.25/7.50/5.20; Queen's Gallery £9.25/8.50/4.65. Combined ticket to Royal Mews and Queen's Gallery £15.75/14.50/9. Royal Day Out ticket (access to all three) £32/29.25/18.20. ⏰ State Rooms open daily late July to Oct daily 9:30am-6:30pm. Last admission 4:15pm. Royal Mews open Apr-Oct daily 10am-5pm; Nov-Dec 22 10am-4pm; Feb-Mar M-Sa 10am-4pm. Last entry Apr-Oct 4:15pm; Nov-Dec 22 and Feb-Mar 3:15pm. Queen's Gallery open daily 10am-5:30pm. Last entry 4:30pm. Open daily late July-Oct.

THE SOUTH BANK

With its warren of cobblestoned streets and picturesque views of the Tower and Tower Bridge, just strolling through the South Bank is an experience. Much of the neighborhood capitalizes on this feeling, with establishments like the London Dungeon and the Clink Prison Museum ready to take you back in time to the neighborhood's less savory past. And who can forget the **London Eye?** We're not sure if the view is worth £17 (just crane your neck at the window when your plane is landing), but it's certainly a staple of the London tourist experience.

🎨 Tate Modern

MUSEUM, MODERN ART

53 Bankside

☎020 7887 8008; www.tate.org.uk

It's hard to believe that you can see all this incredible art for free. Located in George Gilbert Scott's old Brutalist Bankside Power Station (the entrance hall is a magnificent example of grand industrial architecture), Tate Modern defies traditional methods, organizing itself thematically rather than chronologically. The permanent collection sits on two floors, with rotating special exhibits sandwiched in the middle. If you're searching for one work in particular, check out the computers on the fifth floor to scan through the entire collection. Level 3 houses the **Material Gestures** gallery, which focuses on post-war European and American art with gritty, textural works by Claude Monet, Francis Bacon, and Jackson Pollock. Sculptures by Giacometti can also be found here. **Poetry and Dream,** meanwhile, presents themes associated with Surrealism, including the fluid art of Dalí and Picasso. On Level 5, **Energy and Process** looks at Arte Povera, the movement from the 1970s in which everyday materials and natural laws were used to create art; other fancily named genres like post-minimalism and anti-form are also included. **States of Flux** focuses on Cubism and Futurism, among other important modern movements, and presents works by Roy Lichtenstein, Robert Frank, Andy Warhol, and Marcel Duchamp.

▸ ⇄ ⊖Southwark. Turn left onto Blackfriars Rd., right onto Southwark St., left onto Sumner, and finally left onto Holland St. $ Free. Tickets for special exhibits vary; often around £15. Multimedia guide £4, concessions £3.50. ⏰ Open M-Th 10am-6pm, F-Sa 10am-10pm, Su 10am-6pm. Free guided tours of each permanent gallery 11am, noon, 2, and 3pm. 10min talks F and Sa 1pm.

👍 Imperial War Museum — MUSEUM

Lambeth Rd.

☎020 7416 5000; www.iwm.org.uk

Housed in what was once the infamous Bedlam insane asylum, the Imperial War Museum is mad for history. The exhibits start out with two massive naval guns standing sentinel over the imposing building's entrance. The first room is cluttered with enough war-making machinery to make any general salivate. Highlights include a Polaris A3 Missile, the first submarine-launched missile, a full-size German V2 Rocket, and the shell of a "Little Boy," the type of atomic bomb detonated above Hiroshima. Luckily, the bomb is non-functional, but it's still disconcerting when kids whack the casing. The third floor houses a haunting, expansive Holocaust exhibition, which traces the catastrophic injustice of WWII Nazi atrocities with cartographic precision, its miles of film exploring everything from the rhetoric of the Nazi party to the history of anti-Semitism. If this subject matter is too light for your fancy, take solace in the Crimes Against Humanity video exhibition one floor down. The first floor houses the exciting, if sensational, "Secret War" exhibit of WWII spy gadgetry, which provides a brief history of MI5 and the Special Operations Executive. Art nuts will enjoy the museum's unique art collection, called "Breakthrough." The ground floor is devoted to the World Wars, with artifacts, models, videos, and the popular Blitz Experience and Trench Experience exhibits that recreate the feeling of hiding during an air raid and living in the trenches. Also down here is a section on post-1945 conflicts, sure to make you feel chipper about the state of the world.

▸ ⇆ ⊖Lambeth North. Exit the station and walk down Kennington Rd., left onto Lambeth Rd. [$] Free. Special exhibits £6, students £5. Multimedia guides £4.50. ⏰ Open daily 10am-6pm. The Blitz Experience daily schedule is downstairs; it lasts around 10min.

Design Museum MUSEUM

Shad Thames

☎020 7940 8790; www.designmuseum.org

There's something quietly inspirational about this museum, in that it's full of objects that have been designed to make everyday life a little bit prettier, easier, or more fun. The museum doesn't house a permanent collection but rather fills its two floors with rotating exhibits. These tend to focus on things like retrospectives of particular designer's work or collections of the year's most innovative designs from around the world. If you find the incessant parade of paintings and sculptures at other museums a bit boring, come here to find collections of posters, bikes, chairs, video games, and fashion. The galleries themselves are, of course, also impeccably designed in gleaming whites to offset the bright and quirky pieces.

▸ ⇆ ⊖Tower Hill. Cross Tower Bridge. Turn left onto Queen Elizabeth St., then left onto Shad Thames. [$] £11, concessions £10, students £7. ⏰ Open daily 10am-5:45pm. Last entry 5:15pm.

Shakespeare's Globe THEATER, HISTORICAL SITE

21 New Globe Walk

☎020 7902 1500; www.shakespearesglobe.com

The original Globe Theatre burned down during a performance of *Henry VIII* in 1613—whose idea was it to fire a real cannon toward a thatched roof, anyway? Shakespeare's Globe is a recreation of the unique open-air theater, with numerous exhibits and a tour on the history of Shakespeare and London theater. Though short on actual artifacts, the historical overview is fascinating and well designed, and brings to life the bustle and debauchery of the 16th-century South Bank. You'll leave here wondering how the area looked back in the days when bear-baiting was people's idea of a good time. Special booths allow visitors to speak lines with automated casts, and others enable visitors to listen to iconic Shakespearean monologues read by famous actors; check out the one devoted to *Hamlet* to see if you prefer Kenneth Branagh's or Peter O'Toole's rendition of "To be or not to be..." For information on productions, see **Arts and Culture.** Tours of the nearby Rose, an excavated archaeological site of an earlier theater, are also available.

▶ ⚇ ⊖Southwark. Turn left onto Blackfriars Rd., right onto Southwark St., left onto Great Guildford, right onto Park St., left onto Emerson St. The entrance faces the river, around the corner from the main entrance to the theater. Ⓢ Exhibition and Globe tour £11.50, students and seniors £10. Exhibition and Rose tour £9/7.50. ⏰ Exhibition open daily 10am-5pm. Globe tours Apr-Oct 9am-noon. Rose tours Apr-Oct noon-5pm.

SOUTH KENSINGTON AND CHELSEA

🔲 Victoria and Albert Museum   MUSEUM
Cromwell Rd.

☎020 7942 2000; www.vam.ac.uk

The V and A is one of the most all-encompassing museums out there, with a truly memorable collection of beautiful things from across time and space. Founded in 1852 to promote different design ideas to the British public, the museum has examples of styles from around the world. Unlike many museums that feature such a global collection, the V and A is as much about the making of things as it is about the artifacts themselves. The Asia gallery features everything from ornate, gold Buddhist shrines to traditional suits of armor; especially popular is the beautiful Iranian Ardabil Carpet (only lit for 10min. per hr.). The Europe gallery features the enormous (11m by 10.5m) Gothic Revival Hereford Screen that depicts Christ's Ascension, while the British galleries showcase the ever-popular Great Bed of Ware, a 16th-century bed big enough to sleep 15 people. The stained-glass collection on the third floor is another highlight. Those looking for education on the arts should visit the Lecture Theatre or the famous National Art Library, which houses some of Charles Dickens's manuscripts and Leonardo da Vinci's sketches. When you enter the main

Sights

rotunda, don't miss the Rotunda Chandelier by Dale Chihuly right above you.

▶ ⇟ ⊖South Kensington. Turn right onto Thurloe Pl. and left onto Exhibition Rd. The museum is to the right across Cromwell Rd. $ Free. Special exhibitions generally £6-10. ⏰ Open M-Th 10am-5:45pm, F 10am-10pm, Sa-Su 10am-5:45pm. National Art Library open Tu-Th 10am-5:30pm, F 10am-6:30pm, Sa 10am-5:30pm. Free daily tours available; check screens at entrances for times.

Coming Up Roses

Every spring, central London hosts the Chelsea Flower Show, one of the most famous gardening shows in the world. It's impressive even in the likely event that plants aren't really your thing. Stop by to smell the roses in one of the romantic garden pavilions or venture through a tropical wonderland in an expansive rainforest of trumpet trees, yerba mate, and sweet potato plants. The show usually takes place in the last week of May, and you can check the Royal Horticultural Society's website (www.rhs.org.uk) for tickets.

✎ Saatchi Art Gallery — ART GALLERY

Duke of York Sq.

☎020 7811 3085; www.saatchigallery.co.uk

It's rare to find a free gallery of this caliber. The rooms are cavernous and bright, providing ample space for each installation. The gallery focuses on contemporary art from Charles Saatchi's collection. Check out the shop, where many of the works are condensed into pocket-sized forms. There are a few shows every year, with pieces like paintings, sculptures, LED light constructions, and frightening plaster people hunched in corners. Most rooms only have one or two pieces, giving you plenty of space to roam and observe the weird art from all angles—because you know the disaffected art students who work as security guards will judge you if you spent less than 10min. staring at each piece.

▶ ⇟ ⊖Sloane Sq. Go straight out of the Tube and continue onto King's Rd. The square is on the left. $ Free as the wind. ⏰ Open daily 10am-5:45pm.

St Mary Abbots — CHURCH

High St. Kensington

☎020 7937 5136; www.stmaryabbotschurch.org

This gorgeous and silent church sits on a site where Christians have worshipped for 1000 years. It's quite a shock to step off the busy High St. into its stony calm. Designed in 1873 by Victorian architect Sir George Gilbert, the church is known for its stained glass by Clayton and Bell and the scorch marks of the 1944 bombing that are visible in the pews. Musicians from the Royal Academy of Music perform for free on Fridays from 1-2pm

▶ ⇆ ⊖High St. Kensington. Turn right onto Kensington High St. and left onto Kensington Church St. $ Free. ⏰ Open M-Tu 8:30am-6pm, W-F 7:10am-6pm, Sa 9:40am-6pm, Su 8am-6pm.

National Army Museum

MUSEUM

Royal Hospital Rd.

☎020 7730 0717; www.nam.ac.uk

Yet another museum with far too many plaster-people for its own good, the National Army Museum answers the question on everybody's mind: what are British soldiers wearing? With funny hats galore, the museum is packed with information on British military operations since 1066. It paints a vivid picture of army life and presents a remarkably nuanced treatment of the political issues surrounding each conflict. The true gems are W. Siborn's 420 sq. ft., 172-year-old model of the battle of Waterloo and the skeleton of Marengo, Napoleon's favorite horse. Of course, there's the colo(u)ring station and the guns that you can "load" and "fire," but if you want to see what a real gun is like, you might have to wrestle one off an actual guard.

▶ ⇆ ⊖Sloane Sq. Turn left onto Lower Sloane St. and right onto Royal Hospital Rd. $ Free. ⏰ Open daily 10am-5:30pm.

Chelsea Physic Gardens

GARDENS

66 Royal Hospital Rd.

☎020 7352 5646; www.chelseaphysicgarden.co.uk

The Physic Gardens are some of the oldest botanic gardens in Europe. Established in 1673 by a society of apothecaries, the gardens contain pharmaceutical and perfumery plant beds, tropical greenhouses, Europe's oldest rock garden, and a total of 5000 different plants. It's nifty to see plants used to treat everything from heart disease to Alzheimer's, but they're worth a visit for their beauty alone. Witchcraft and wizardry nerds should look for the mandrake roots.

▶ ⇆ ⊖Sloane Sq. Turn left onto Lower Sloane St. and right onto Royal Hospital Rd. ℹ Free guided tours, depending on availability of guides. $ £8, students and children £5, under 5 free. ⏰ Open Apr-Oct W-F noon-5pm, Su noon-6pm.

Sights

Chelsea Old Church

CHURCH

64 Cheyne Walk

☎020 7795 1019; www.chelseaoldchurch.org.uk

Though Chelsea Old Church was bombed like so many others in 1941, its rebuilding was slightly different than most; parishioners simply picked up the destroyed plaques and monuments and put them back together, leaving the cracks to serve as delicate reminders of the war. The church has also hosted several celebrity worshippers. Henry VIII is rumored to have married Jane Seymour here; Queen Elizabeth I, "Bloody" Mary, and Lady Jane Gray worshipped here; and Thomas More prayed in the chapel that is named after him.

▶ 🪧 ⊖ Sloane Sq. Turn left onto Lower Sloane St., right onto Royal Hospital Rd., and right onto Cheyne Walk. $ Free. ⏰ Open Tu-Th 2-4pm, Su for services (Holy Communion 8am and 12:15pm, children's service 10am, Mattins 11am, Evensong 6pm).

Brompton Oratory

CHURCH

Brompton Rd.

☎020 7808 0900; www.bromptonoratory.com

Built between 1880 and 1884, the Brompton Oratory is named after its founders, the Oratorians. Its breathtaking nave is wider than the one in St. Paul's. The marble-packed Catholic church is filled with Baroque flourishes, as well as Soviet secrets: the KGB used it as a drop point for secret messages during the Cold War.

▶ 🪧 ⊖Knightsbridge. Turn left onto Brompton Rd. $ Free. ⏰ Open daily 6:30am-8pm. Services M-F 7, 8, 10am, 12:30, 6pm (in Latin); Sa 7, 8, 10am, 6pm; Su 8, 9, 10, 11am (Latin), 12:30, 4:30, 7pm.

Natural History Museum

MUSEUM

Cromwell Rd.

☎020 7942 5011; www.nhm.ac.uk

Sure, the museum may be intended for kids—cue the roving school groups—but who doesn't love a moving T-Rex? Known as the "Cathedral of the Animals," the Natural History Museum houses exhibitions on everything from animal anatomy to histories of scientific research. Though the dinosaurs rule, there are also exhibits on every type of animal, plant, and ecosystem—the Darwin Centre features more than 20 million species in jars. The grand Victorian building, with turrets and gargoyles galore, is enough to make the visit worthwhile.

▶ 🪧 ⊖South Kensington. Turn right onto Thurloe Pl. and left onto Exhibition

Rd. The museum is to the left across Cromwell Rd. *i* Book early for tours of Darwin's special collections. Ⓢ Free. Special exhibits around £8; students get discounts. 🕐 Open daily 10am-5:50pm. Last entry 5:30pm.

Kensington Palace   PALACE

Kensington Palace Gardens

☎0844 482 7777; www.hrp.org.uk/kensingtonpalace

This elegant royal residence was begun in the 17th century and expanded by the legendary architect Sir Christopher Wren. It's long been home to monarchs and other nobility, though it was never the official seat of the court. Queen Victoria and the princes William and Harry grew up here. Even though Will is now taken (he and the Duchess of Cambridge use the palace as their official London residence), princess hopefuls can still catch sight of Harry during his occasional visits. The majority of the palace is closed until construction is completed in 2012, but the State Rooms have been transformed into an "Enchanted Palace" exhibit, which features a story about seven of the legendary princesses who lived here. The exhibit threads through many magnificent galleries and drawing rooms done up in an eerie, fairy-tale style with a soundtrack to match.

▶ ⚐ ⊖High St. Kensington. Turn right leaving the station and head down the road, then enter the park and make for the palace (it's kind of hard to miss). Ⓢ £12.50, concessions £11, under 16 £6.25. 🕐 Open daily 10am-6pm.

HYDE PARK TO NOTTING HILL

It's pretty hard to be in central London and not run into ⬛**Hyde Park** at some point—the park is larger than the entire principality of Monaco. The land was first converted into a park by Henry VIII in the 16th century. Since then, it's developed from a royal deer park into open public space. Technically the roughly rectangular area of greenery here comprises both Hyde Park and Kensington Gardens (the latter is the western part, closer to Notting Hill), but you'll barely notice the difference except for the fact that Hyde Park closes at midnight while the other shuts its gates at dusk. The parks are full of winding pathways, open fields, floral gardens, and small clusters of woods. Since Hyde Park has been around for nearly 500 years, there are also a number of interesting historical sites for those who want more than just greenery.

Sights

Speakers' Corner

HISTORICAL SITE, PERFORMANCE SPACE

Hyde Park, Park Ln.

This innocuous corner of Hyde Park is the stage for political, religious, and social debates. Speakers present ideas, challenge each other, and take questions from the audience (some regular hecklers hang out in the area). Back in the day, it was used by social revolutionaries like Marx, Lenin, and George Orwell; today you're as likely to find a fundamentalist Christian as a **Communist**. There are no set hours, and anyone is welcome to speak, though sometimes the area remains empty. Come watch free speech in action!

▶ Marble Arch. Go through the arch into the park and the area where most people speak is the paved section between the arch and the beginning of the main grassy area. $ Free. ⏰ Hours vary, but around 9am-10pm in summer.

Serpentine Boating Lake

LAKE BOATING

Hyde Park

☎020 7262 1330; www.theboathouselondon.co.uk

Built from 1727 to 1731 in memory of Queen Caroline, the Serpentine Boating Lake is one of the most beautiful parts of Hyde Park. Rented boats drift lazily across the placid waters as fat waterfowl battle it out for pieces of bread. Boats can be rented and taken out for any amount of time. The water stretches across a large portion of the park; at the Bayswater end is a terraced bit with fountains—refined British landscapery at its best.

▶ Hyde Park Corner. $ Pedal boats and row boats £8 per person per 30min., £10 per person per hr. ⏰ Open daily Easter-October10am-sundown.

Subway Gallery

GALLERY

Joe Strummer Subway

☎078 1128 6503; www.subwaygallery.com

Bringing a new meaning to the term "underground art" (their joke, not ours), the Subway Gallery features installations from local artists, often dealing with pop culture and music. The main spot is in a tiny kiosk, though pop graffiti adorns the walls of the underpass. Exhibits change monthly. If you're in the area (or a huge fan of the Clash), it's definitely worth stopping by this very cool, quirky venue. At night, though, it might feel deserted and a bit dangerous.

▶ Edgware Rd. Take a sharp right down Cabbell St., left before the flyover and then go down the stairs into Joe Strummer Subway. $ Free. ⏰ Open M-Sa 11am-7pm.

Apsley House

HISTORICAL SITE, MUSEUM GALLERY

Hyde Park Corner

☎020 7499 5676; www.english-heritage.org.uk

Named for Baron Apsley, the house later known as "No.1, London" was bought by the Duke of Wellington in 1817 (his heirs still occupy a modest suite on the top floor). The house is a stunning architectural triumph, from the gilded mirrors to the oval spiral staircase. Perhaps the most fantastic of all the valuable collections in the house is Wellington's art collection, much of which he received from grateful European monarchs after he defeated Napoleon at the Battle of Waterloo. One of the most sought-after pieces is Velázquez's beautiful *The Water-Seller of Seville.* Throughout the house, you can find various pretty awesome collectibles, including a silver-gilt dessert plate bearing Napoleon's arms, the key to the city of Pamplona (granted after the Duke captured the city), the death masks of Wellington and Napoleon, and a stunning 6.7m Egyptian service set given by Napoleon to Josephine as a divorce present. Scholars maintain that the dessert service was meant as a mean joke about Josephine's weight—it's huge. Unless you're particularly interested in English history or Portuguese silverwork, though, it may not be worth the price of admission given that so many other museums and galleries in the city are free.

▶ ♯ ⊖Hyde Park Corner. *i* June 18 is Wellington Day, so check for special events. Ⓢ £6.30, concessions £5.70, children £3.80. Joint ticket with Wellington Arch £7.90/7.10/4.70. Audio tour free. ⏰ Open Apr-Oct W-Su 11am-5pm, Nov-Mar W-Su 11am-4pm. Last entry 30min. before close.

MARYLEBONE AND BLOOMSBURY

With the **British Museum** and the **British Library** just a 15min. walk from each other, you've got basically the whole empire packed into this one little area (eh, we guess you'd want Buckingham Palace and Westminster in there too if you were going to be really thorough about it). **Regent's Park** is one of the loveliest expanses of green in London, and all the streets surrounding the park have stunning architecture that makes a perfect continuation of your stroll around the verge. **University College London** is located along Gower St.—its main campus and the red-brick Cruciform building (once the old teaching hospital) are worth a gander.

British Museum

MUSEUM

Great Russell St.

☎020 7323 8299; www.british-museum.org

Ah, colonialism. It's a bummer about the whole exploitation and oppression thing, but, man, does it make for some awesome souvenirs. Nowhere is this clearer than the British Museum, founded in 1753 as the personal collection of Sir Hans Sloane. Nowadays, the museum juxtaposes Victorian Anglocentricism with more modern, multicultural acceptance, but there's no way you won't be reminded of the fact that back when this place was built, the sun never set on the British Empire. The building itself, in all its Neoclassical splendor, is magnificent. The stunning **Great Court** is the largest covered square in Europe, and has been used as the British Library stacks for the past 150 years. The blue chairs and desks of the **Reading Room,** set under a towering dome of books, have shouldered the weight of research by almost every major British writer, as well as Marx, Lenin, and Trotsky.

The collection is organized by geographic region: Greece and Rome, Egypt and Sudan, the Middle East, Britain and Europe, etc. Most of the extremely famous pieces, like the **Rosetta Stone** and the **Elgin Marbles,** are located on the ground floor. However, don't miss out on the galleries above; the Early Britain collection is particularly fine, with intensely detailed artifacts that are hard to imagine coming from muddy Dark Ages-era England.

Look out for the **King's Library** on the eastern part of the ground floor, which holds artifacts gathered from throughout the world by English explorers during the Enlightenment. Some of the central display cases bear descriptions, but much of the collection is jumbled together without explanation—a curatorial choice meant to recreate the feel of collections from the period. We think it works pretty well. Mixed in with the artifacts are shelves full of books from the House of Commons' library—get your dork on and try to find an 18th-century copy of your favorite Roman poet or Greek historian.

▸ ⇟ ⊖ Tottenham Court Rd., Russell Sq., or Holborn. ℹ Tours by request. $ £4 suggested donation. Prices for events and special exhibitions vary, most £8-12. Excellent color maps with self-guided tours £2. Multimedia guide £5. ⏰ Museum open daily 10am-5:30pm. Select exhibitions M-W 10am-5:30pm, Th-F 10am-8:30pm, Sa-Su 10am-5:30pm.

Sights

British Library

LIBRARY

96 Euston Rd.

☎020 7412 7676; www.bl.uk

Though it was castigated during its long construction by traditionalists for being too modern and by modernists for being too traditional, the new British Library building (opened in 1998) now impresses all nay-sayers with its stunning interior. The 65,000 volumes of the King's Library, collected by George III and bequeathed to the nation in 1823 by his less bookish son, George IV, are displayed in a glass cube toward the rear. The sunken plaza out front features an enormous and somewhat strange statue of Newton, and also hosts a series of free concerts and other events. The heart of the library is underground, with 12 million books on 200 miles of shelving. The above-ground brick building is home to cavernous reading rooms and an engrossing museum. Find **Shakespeare's first folio,** Lewis Carroll's handwritten manuscript of *Alice in Wonderland* (donated by Alice Liddell herself), and Virginia Woolf's handwritten notes for *Mrs. Dalloway* (then called *The Hours*) in the **Literature Corner** of the Sir John Ritblat Gallery. Music-lovers will appreciate Handel's handwritten *Messiah,* Mozart's marriage contract, Beethoven's tuning fork, and a whole display dedicated to the Beatles. The last of these includes the original, handwritten lyrics to "A Hard Day's Night," scrawled on the back of Lennon's son Julian's first birthday card. In the museum, the original copy of the **Magna Carta** has its own room (accompanied by the Papal Bull that Pope Innocent III wrote in response). Leonardo da Vinci's notebooks are in the **Science** section, while one of 50 known **Gutenberg Bibles** can be found in the **Printing** section. Another gallery hosts temporary exhibitions that dig up more gems from the Library's collection, often mixed in with interviews from authors and artists. Even if you don't crack a book during your entire stay in London, you'll still feel at least 10 IQ points smarter just from being around all this knowledge.

▶ ⚐ ⊖ Euston Sq. or King's Cross St. Pancras. *i* Free Wi-Fi; the cafe offers lots of seating where you can take advantage of it. To register for use of reading room, bring 2 forms of ID—1 with a signature and 1 with a home address. $ Free. Tours free. Group tour up to 15 people, £85. ⏰ Open M 9:30am-6pm, Tu 9:30am-8pm, W-F 9:30am-6pm, Sa 9:30am-5pm, Su 11am-5pm. Group tours Tu 10:30am and 2:30pm, Th 10:30am and 2:30pm. Call ☎020 7412 7639 to book. Individual tours M, W, F 11am. Call ☎019 3754 6546 to book.

Abbey Road

London has numerous pilgrimage sites for music fanatics, but few can compare with six thick stripes in St John's Wood, a little west of Regent's Park. Located near EMI's Abbey Road Studios at 3 Abbey Rd., this zebra crossing was vaulted into iconic status by the Beatles' final album, *Abbey Road.* For the album's cover, John, Ringo, Paul, and George strode across the southeastern edge of the street and onto the to-do list of every tourist who saw them standing there. If you've grown out some happening facial hair and slipped on your hippest pair of bell-bottoms, feel free to pose like it's 1969. But please be quick; busy Londoners driving their cars don't appreciate day trippers on magical mystery tours trying to decide whether or not to do it in the road.

▓ The Regent's Park   PARK

☎020 7486 7905; www.royalparks.org.uk

In 1811, the Prince Regent commissioned John Nash to design him a private garden; the park was opened to the public in 1841, and the city lives all the better for it. Locals, pigeons, and tourists alike frolic among the 10,000 wild flowers and 50 acres of pitches and courts. **Queen Mary's Garden** houses the national collection of delphiniums and a gorgeous collection of 30,000 roses. It is also home to an interesting strain of pink flower known as **Sexy Rexy.** The park's popular open-air theater is the setting for all kinds of shows (book tickets at www.openairtheatre.com). The **Gardens of St. John's Lodge,** behind one of the park's eight villas, serve as a place for quiet meditation beneath gorgeous latticed archways—a sort of secret garden that also affords a peek into the back of St. John's Lodge. Be aware that security here is tight; the **Winfield House** just off the outer circle is home to the American ambassador. In the northern section of the park is the **London Zoo** (www. zsl.org), home to all sorts of critters and, in summertime, a giant penguin pool.

▶ ‡ ⊖Regent's Park. Ⓢ Deck chair £1.50 per hr., £4 per 3hr., £7 per day. Boats £6.50 per 1hr., £4.85 per 1½hr. Zoo £20, concessions £19, children £16. ⏲ Park open daily 5am-dusk. Boating lake open daily Mar-Oct 10:30am-7pm. Zoo open daily 10am-5:30pm.

Sights

NORTH LONDON

🏛 Hampstead Heath   PARK

Hampstead
☎020 7332 3030

Hampstead Heath was initially much smaller than its present 800 acres. After Sir Thomas Maryon Wilson tried to develop and sell off the Heath in the early 19th century, the public fought to keep the Heath wild; an 1872 Act of Parliament declared it open to the public forever. Now it sprawls gloriously in the heart of Hampstead, feeling much wilder and lusher than the manicured parks of central London. The beautiful, tamer **Hill Gardens** are in the southwest corner of the Heath just off North End Ave., created out of the surrounding landscapes by Lord Leverhulme (of Lever Soap fame). For a stunning sunset view, look through the pergola with Georgian columns and rose-entwined lattice. **Parliament Hill** is one of the highest points in London, offering those willing to climb its deceptively steep sides a glorious reminder that they're only four miles from London proper, not in the middle of rural England. Parliament Hill derives its name from its use as a point of defense for Parliamentarian "Roundheads" during the English Civil War—though legend has it that Guy Fawkes planned to watch Parliament explode from the hill.

▶ 🚌 Bus #210 will drop you at the north of the Heath. Alternatively, get off at ⊖Hampstead, turn right onto Heath St., go up North End Way, left onto Inverforth Close, and left onto a path to arrive at the hill gardens. Bus #214 allows easy access to Parliament Hill. ⏰ Heath open 24hr. Hill Garden open daily May 24-Aug 1 8:30am-8:30pm; Aug 2-May 23 8:30am-1hr. before sunset.

Kenwood House   GALLERY

Hampstead Ln.
☎020 8348 1286; www.english-heritage.org.uk

Lord Iveagh, a barrister and Lord Chief Justice, lived here in the 18th century. Visitors to Kenwood House can now admire his fabulous art collection and see how the 18th-century elite lived. Iveagh's bequest fills the house with paintings that are essentially odes to the London of yore. Views of the city from the Heath, like Crone's *View of London from Highgate,* and an early Turner depict themes common to the bequest—typical British life. Though they aren't British, the stars of the

collection are probably Rembrandt's *Portrait of the Artist* and
Vermeer's *The Guitar Player.* The Suffolk Collection, com-
posed mainly of portraits, is on semi-permanent exhibition
on the first floor. Concerts are held in the grounds during
the summer.

▶ 🚌 Bus #210 stops on Hampstead Ln. at the Kenwood House stop. The
park is across the road. 💲 Free. Booklets £4. 🕙 Open daily 11:30am-4pm.
Last entry 3:50pm.

EAST LONDON

🖾 Whitechapel Gallery   GALLERY

77-82 Whitechapel High St.

☎020 7522 7888; www.whitechapelgallery.org

In business since 1901, the Whitechapel Gallery was originally
an effort by hoity-toity uppity-ups to bring art to the culturally
deprived inhabitants of the East End. Today, the gallery's atmosphere has changed, but its commitment to excellence remains.
Gallery 7 is dedicated to temporary exhibits (which change
four times per year), Gallery 2 features year-long commissioned
works, and the rest of the gallery is filled with other contemporary works, as well as occasional mid-career retrospectives. Art
films run on loop in the cinema space.

▶ 🚇 ⊖Aldgate East. Turn left on Whitechapel High St. 💲 Free. Special exhibits normally under £10, students £2 discount. 🕙 Open Tu-Su 11am-6pm,
1st Th of every month 11am-9pm.

🖾 Geffrye Museum   MUSEUM

136 Kingsland Rd.

☎020 7739 9893; www.geffrye-museum.org.uk

At first glance, the Geffrye is yet another house-turned-
museum, but if the thought of looking at upholstery for an hour
has you cringing, think again. The museum consists of several
old almshouses arranged around a pretty garden. Inside, walk
through a series of 17th- to 21st-century living rooms, whose
changing styles do a remarkably good job of eking out social,
cultural, and political themes—who knew you could learn so
much from a chair? Special exhibits often feature model living
spaces from other cultures.

▶ 🚇 ⊖Hoxton. Make a right onto Geffrye St., a left onto Pearson St., and a
left onto Kingsland Rd. 💲 Free. Special exhibits around £5. 🕙 Open Tu-Sa
10am-5pm, Su noon-5pm.

Ripperology

Whether you're a big fan of Wikipedia's list of serial killers or too afraid to watch commercials for *Dexter,* you've probably heard of Jack the Ripper. Believed to have been responsible for at least five and up to 11 murders in the Whitechapel area east of central London, the killer caused quite a splash in the press, thanks in great part to his gruesome methods—he usually slashed the throat, mutilated the face and genitals, and removed the internal organs of his victim. The policemen and various newspapers received letters from people claiming to be responsible, one of which included half a human kidney, and the claim that the writer had "fried and ate" the other half. The name "Jack the Ripper" comes from one of these letters; less catchy nicknames offered at the time include "The Whitechapel Murderer," "Leather Apron," and "Nigel the Ripper."

Of course, the most interesting thing about Jack the Ripper is that he was never caught or even identified. Before you start panicking, remember that these murders took place in 1888—meaning it's really Dexter, not Jack, you should be worried about. If you're still itching to learn more, a number of tour companies (try www.jack-the-ripper-tour.com or www.thejacktherippertour.com) offer tours with no shortage of grizzly details.

Royal Observatory
HISTORIC SITE, MUSEUM

Blackheath Ave.

☎020 8312 6608; www.nmm.ac.uk

Charles II founded the Royal Observatory in 1675 to "advance navigation and astronomy." Translation: to stop British ships from sinking so frequently. The observatory is at Greenwich, the site of the Prime Meridian (or longitude 0° 0'0"), which demarcates the boundary between the Eastern and Western hemispheres. If your visit to London hasn't yet demonstrated the sheer power of the British Empire, this should—once upon a time, the British got to decide how time worked. Visitors can pose for pictures straddling the red LED strip, thus standing in two hemispheres simultaneously. After seeing this intersection, visitors choose one of two routes. One explores the history of the observatory and its research, while the other focuses on astrology and leads to the popular planetarium.

Sights

▶ ✝ ⊖Greenwich. Turn left onto Kay Way, right down Straightsmouth to Greenwich High Rd., right onto Stockwell St., left onto Nevada St., then left onto King William Walk. Finally, take a right onto Romney Rd. and walk up the hill. *i* Handicapped tourists should know that, while there is parking on top of the hill, the hill itself is very steep. Ⓢ £10, concessions £7.50. Planetarium shows £6.50/4.50. Audio tour £3.50. Guided tours free. Ⓣ Open daily 10am-5pm.

SOUTH LONDON

South London Gallery   ART GALLERY
65 Peckham Rd.
☎020 7703 6120; www.southlondonartgallery.org

This tiny art gallery attracts as many visitors with its lively cafe as it does with its two exhibition spaces. It showcases works by artists of all sorts—established, up-and-coming, British, international, you name it. There are events like talks and film screenings here, and many are free. With so much art in London, the out-of-the-way location means this gallery isn't really a must-see, but, if you're in the area, it's worth stopping by to take a peek at the interesting art and the lovely 19th-century building.

▶ ✝ ⊖Peckham Rye. Bus 37 goes from the station to the gallery. Ⓢ Free. Ⓣ Open Tu 11am-6pm, W 11am-9pm, Th-Su 11am-6pm.

WEST LONDON

◪ Hampton Court Palace   PALACE
East Molesey, Surrey
☎0844 482 7777; www.hrp.org.uk/hamptoncourtpalace

If you're a fan of the Tudors (either the historical figures or the saucy Showtime television series), the lavish Hampton Court is a must-see. It was originally built by Cardinal Wolsey to be his own palace while he was in the good graces of Henry VIII, but he gave it to the king in a last-ditch effort to prevent his downfall. Henry added vast kitchens and the magnificent Great Hall where he dined in style (and where Shakespeare's theater company later performed). Mary I spent her honeymoon here, and Elizabeth I used the palace as well. Each monarch added his or her own touches, which can be seen in the variety of architectural styles, from medieval gates to faux-Versailles frippery.

It remained a royal residence until the early 18th century. Visitors can see many of the royal apartments, grand rooms like the Chapel Royal, and the extensive kitchens (which had to feed 1200 people every day). While the rooms are visually stunning and packed with art, the real draw is that the palace uses interactive exhibits and informative guides to give a genuine feel for what life was like within its walls. Don't be limited by those walls, though, as there are 750 acres of impeccably maintained grounds to stroll. These include the Privy Garden, the Rose Garden, the Exotics Garden, and—if all the perfectly manicured grass and topiaries are driving you crazy—a 20th-century garden done in a more "informal" style. Best of all, there is a world-famous maze that will put your navigational skills to the test.

▶ ✈ Trains run from Waterloo to Hampton Court (£5.50). The palace is just across the bridge from the train station. 𝒊 Audio and guided tours included with admission. Ⓢ Gardens £5.30, concessions £5, children free. Maze £3.85, children £2.75. Combined ticket £16, concessions £13, children under 16 £8. ⏰ Open daily 10am-6pm. Last entry to garden 5pm; last entry to maze 5:15pm.

Royal Botanic Gardens, Kew   BOTANICAL GARDENS
Richmond, Surrey
☎020 8332 5000; www.kew.org

Kew Gardens make most other botanical gardens look like suburban backyards. This is one of the foremost botanical research facilities in the world, home to thousands of plant species and hundreds of scientists who tend to them. Perhaps more relevant to the casual visitor, it has exquisite gardens, winding paths through leafy forests and rolling lawns, and conservatories with collections of everything from orchids to carnivorous plants. There's even a skywalk that takes you through the tree canopy. If you prefer buildings to shrubberies, you can check out the many interesting architectural specimens: Swiss-style cottages, faux-Chinese pagodas, one of the smaller royal palaces, and several galleries and museums with plant-related art and information.

▶ ✈ ⊖Kew Gardens. Exit the station and walk down Litchfield Rd. to the gardens' Victoria Gate. Ⓢ £13.90, concessions £11.90, under 17 free. Kew Palace £5.30/4.50/free. ⏰ Open M-F 9:30am-6:30pm, Sa-Su 9:30am-7:30pm. Last entry 30min. before close. Glasshouses and galleries daily 9:30am-5:30pm. Free guided tours leave Victoria Plaza at 11am and 2pm.

Food

British food doesn't have a great reputation. Yes, it is bad for you and no, it doesn't have complex flavors, but it is so intrinsically a part of British life that to forego it would be a grave error for any visitor. Fish and chips, bangers and mash, tikka masala (a British invention), and warm ale are all different names for the same thing: comfort food. Neighborhoods like Brixton and Shoreditch serve up a span of ethnic cuisine, from Caribbean to Indian, while gourmet restaurants whip up inventive dishes. "Pub grub" still rules over everything. In case you hadn't noticed, Brits like to operate in certain set ways. There's a reason that old war propaganda line, "Keep Calm and Carry On," is plastered all over the place; there's a reason the Queen still rolls down the Mall every June; there's a reason the Brits always think England will win the Cup; there's a reason fair Albion still uses the pound; and for that same reason, you'll always be able to get a pie and a pint on any corner in London. Now eat your mushy peas—the cod's getting cold.

Budget Food

In London, the budget traveler faces the same dilemma as she does in America and other takeout societies—save your wallet or save your cholesterol. Most cheap food in London, though delicious, is of the fried and heart-attack-inducing variety. But by god, it is delicious. Head to the area between Hyde Park and Notting Hill for the best deals on these greasy delicacies. For those looking for a balanced meal, the South Bank has all the staples minus the large price tags.

THE CITY OF LONDON

Many of the culinary offerings in the City are geared toward businessmen (expensive) and tourists (expensive, but not very good). Fortunately, if you know where to look, this neighborhood also holds some of London's best eats. The area around **Clerkenwell** overflows with creative and delicious restaurants, pubs, and cafes.

🍴 City Càphê — VIETNAMESE $

17 Ironmonger Ln.
www.citycaphe.com

If you want a cheap yet delicious sandwich, try one of the exquisite bánh mì at this simple Vietnamese joint. Slices of pork, chicken, or tofu are served with salad and dressing on baguettes, which are baked using a closely guarded secret recipe. We don't know how a pork sandwich with some salad on a white baguette can be so good, so if you have any ideas, let us know. Pho, rice noodle dishes, and a variety of rolls are also available.

▶ 🪧 ⊖Bank. Head down Poultry away from the stop, then turn right onto Ironmonger Ln. $ Bánh mì £4. Other dishes £4-6. ⏰ Open M-F 11:30am-3pm.

🍴 Coach and Horses — PUB $$

26-28 Ray St.
☎020 7278 8990; www.thecoachandhorses.com

"Pub food" often brings soggy pies and oily fish and chips to mind, but this Victorian pub in a seemingly abandoned corner of Clerkenwell upends these expectations with fresh, inventive takes on British fare. Coach and Horses does have mushy peas, fish and chips, burgers, and the like, but it also has beetroot risotto, heirloom tomato salad, and duck confit. A variety of roasts are served on Sunday. You can eat in their enclosed garden, sidewalk patio, or elegant dining rooms.

▶ 🚏 ⊖Farringdon. Walk north on Farringdon Rd. and turn left onto Ray St. $ Main courses £8-12. 2-course lunch £10. ⏰ Open M-F noon-11pm, Sa 6-11pm, Su 1-5pm. Kitchen open M-F noon-3pm and 6-10pm, Sa 6-10pm, Su 1-4pm.

Bar Battu — MEDITERRANEAN $$

48 Gresham St.

☎020 7036 6100; www.barbattu.com

Primarily known for their all-natural wines (fewer sulfites, less hangover!), Bar Battu serves up some pretty outstanding food as well. Get a selection of charcuterie or a leek tart or go all out with linguini with borlotti beans in a lemon-caper vinaigrette. Bar Battu is one of London's best values for a gourmet meal, with all the impeccable service and classy atmosphere you'd expect, but lower prices and larger portions.

▶ 🚏 ⊖Bank. Go down Prince's St. and turn left onto Gresham St. $ Appetizers and small plates £4.50-6.50. Main courses £9.50-14. 2-course meal £16.25; 3-course £20. ⏰ Open M-F 11:30am-11pm.

The Clerkenwell Kitchen — BRITISH, SEASONAL $$

31 Clerkenwell Close

☎020 7101 9959; www.theclerkenwellkitchen.co.uk

Normally when a restaurant advertises "soft drinks," they mean cola and root beer, but here at the Clerkenwell Kitchen, the term refers to taste-bud-exploding concoctions like their elderflower cordial (£2). Match that with their locally grown ingredients and organic, free-range meat, and you'll have a welcome introduction to the lighter side of British fare. During the summer, bask in the sun outside on the terrace; in the winter, warm up with dishes like slow-roast pork belly with braised lentils, chard, and quince aioli. The menu changes daily based on which fresh, local ingredients they receive, but the high quality of this hidden restaurant is consistent.

▶ 🚏 ⊖Farringdon. Turn right onto Cowcross St., right onto Farringdon Rd., right onto Pear Tree Ct., and right onto Clerkenwell Close. Walk straight as if still on Pear Tree Ct. If you see the church, you've gone too far. $ Main courses £7.50-11. Tea and coffee £1.50-1.85. ⏰ Open M-F 8am-5pm.

Child's Play

Remember singing "London Bridge is Falling Down" as a kid? If this is your first time in the British capital, you might be interested to see the bridge still standing. That's about where the interest will end, as London Bridge is one of the city's most boring river crossings. But the song's ambiguous history might make up for its subject's aesthetic dullness. One theory, going off the parallel between the song and similar verses in a Norse saga, claims the rhyme refers to Norweigian King Olaf II's 11th-century invasion of London and destruction of London Bridge. A slightly less interesting version says that children simply chanted about the deterioration of London Bridge after the Great Fire of London in 1666. The most bizarre theory is also the goriest: some say the song refers to the burial of children inside the foundations of the bridge due to an ancient belief that bridges would collapse without human sacrifice. Hopefully, the fact the bridge was "falling down" refers to the lack of children buried in it, rather than there simply not being enough.

THE WEST END

🍴 Kulu Kulu — SUSHI $$

76 Brewer St.

☎020 7734 7316; www.kulukulu.co.uk

Kulu Kulu is a conveyor-belt sushi restaurant—the chefs send a steady stream of fresh dishes around the bar on a little runway. You can see everything before you order it and try lots of little dishes. Different plates indicate different prices; when you're ready to pay, a waiter will come over and add up your plates. Typical choices are nigiri, sashimi, and maki, and some vegetables and non-sushi dishes. It's a no-frills environment, but one of the best values in the area.

▶ ♿ ⊖Piccadilly Circus. Go down Glasshouse St., keep right onto Sherwood St., and turn left onto Brewer St. $ Dishes £1.50-3.60 (4-5 dishes make a good meal). ⏰ Open M-Sa noon-10pm.

🍴 Freebird Burritos — MEXICAN $

Corner of Ruper St. and Brewer St.

www.freebirdburritos.com

Just a humble food stand, Freebird has one of London's great rarities: a pretty good burrito. It maybe isn't as good as what you'd find in the US (or Mexico, obviously), but it's cheap and a rare find around here.

▶ ⚡ ⊖Piccadilly Circus. Turn right down Shaftesbury Ave. and left onto Rupert St. Ⓢ Burritos £5, with guacamole £5.50. ⏰ Open M-F 11:30am-3pm.

⬛ Monmouth Coffee Company   CAFE $
27 Monmouth St.

☎0872 148 1409; www.monmouthcoffee.co.uk

Monmouth makes the best coffee in London (some say the world, but we still have our researchers working to verify that one). Their carefully selected and roasted beans are served at other establishments in the city, but you should come to the flagship store itself. They use amazingly creamy milk from an organic farm in Somerset, so skip the skim this time. Try their pastries and truffles, too. The shop is small, but there's some seating available on the upper floor.

▶ ⚡ ⊖Leicester Sq. Turn right and then left onto Upper St. Martin's Ln., which becomes Monmouth St. Ⓢ Coffee £1.20-2.50. ⏰ Open M-Sa 8am-6:30pm.

Fortnum and Mason   AFTERNOON TEA, FOOD STORE $$$$
181 Piccadilly

☎020 7734 8040; www.fortnumandmason.com

If you have a bit of extra money to burn and want to experience some classic hoity-toity English elegance, try the afternoon tea at Fortnum and Mason. Not only do you get a whole spread of sandwiches, scones, and cakes, you can sit in luxurious armchairs while being served by a waiter who is too well trained to look askance at your grubby flip-flops (not that we speak from personal experience). If you're going to splurge on one meal in London, it should be at this truly British institution that has been around for over 300 years. If, however, the prices seem a tad too exorbitant, pick up specialty teas, jams, biscuits, and much more at the amazing food store downstairs.

▶ ⚡ ⊖Piccadilly Circus. Turn left down Piccadilly. Ⓢ Afternoon tea £34-40. ⏰ Open M-Sa noon-6:30pm, Su noon-4:30pm. Store open M-Sa 10am-8pm, Su noon-6pm.

WESTMINSTER

🍴 Poilâne — BAKERY $

46 Elizabeth St.

☎020 7808 4910; www.poilane.com

This is the only non-French branch of the famous Parisian bakery chain Poilâne, which means that it's ungodly good by London standards. The commitment to excellence at Poilâne is unparalleled: many of their bakers actually live above the shop, baking the bread all through the night to ensure that it's fresh for the morning crowd. They use the time-honored traditions and techniques when creating their sourdough masterpieces, and the *pain au chocolat* is to die for. Also worth noting, they bake in wood-fired ovens of the type that started the Great Fire of London—good thing the city's not built of wood anymore.

▶ 🚉 ⊖Victoria. Turn left onto Buckingham Palace Rd., then right onto Elizabeth St. [$] Pain au chocolat £1.50. Walnut bread £4. Sourdough bread £5. Custard tart £17. ⏰ Open M-F 7:30am-7pm, Sa 7:30am-6pm.

🍴 Pimlico Fresh — CAFE, MEDITERRANEAN $

86 Wilton Rd.

☎020 7932 0030

If you're stumbling off a train at Victoria, we know pretty much any combination of carbohydrates and protein will probably sound like manna from heaven. But if you're by the station (whether for transportation reasons or not), try and hold out until you're a bit farther down the road. You'll be rewarded by this fabulous bakery and restaurant. Try a baked egg with chorizo or salmon and avocado toast for breakfast; the rest of the day, Pimlico serves lasagna, stews with rice, salad, omelettes, and a number of daily specials. They also serve the ever-popular Monmouth coffee.

▶ 🚉 ⊖Victoria. Wilton Rd. runs behind the station, toward Pimlico, away from Buckingham Palace. *i* Takeaway available. [$] Main courses £4.50-7. Coffee from £1.80. ⏰ Open M-F 7:30am-7:30pm, Sa-Su 9am-6pm.

Bumbles — BRITISH $$

16 Buckingham Palace Rd.

☎020 7828 2903; www.bumbles1950.com

Specializing in highbrow British cuisine and the fine art of the affordable *prix-fixe* menu, Bumbles is an incongruously good value for this part of town. It looks unremarkable from the outside, but is surprisingly elegant within, with white leather chairs and wine-red walls. Dishes include truffled toast, Devonshire lamb, and roasted frogs' leg trifle. Try them in an extremely affordable three-course meal from a limited menu, a two- or three-course choice from the full selection, or go crazy and get the eight-course "Taste of Mr. Bumbles." You can also order a la carte, but where's the fun in that?

▶ 🚏 ⊖Victoria. Exit the station and turn right onto Buckingham Palace Rd. [$] Limited 3-course menu £10; 2 courses £20, 3 courses £23; 8-course menu £39. ⏰ Open M-F noon-3pm and 5-10pm, Sa 5-10pm.

Jenny Lo's Teahouse

ASIAN FUSION $$

14 Eccleston St.

☎020 7259 0399; www.jennylo.co.uk

Want to see how people besides the Brits do tea? This unassuming teahouse serves delicious Asian classics like Vietnamese-style vermicelli rice noodles, Thai-style lamb in green curry, and wok noodles. But they also have their own herbalist (Dr. Xu) and a terrific selection of soothing and tasty teas.

▶ 🚏 ⊖Victoria. Turn left onto Buckingham Palace Rd., then a right onto Eccleston St. ℹ Takeaway and delivery available. [$] Main courses £7.50-9.50. Teas £2-4. Cash only. ⏰ Open M-F noon-3pm and 6-10pm.

THE SOUTH BANK

The South Bank is home to the terrific **Borough Market.** Located just south of London Bridge, it's a tangle of stalls and shops where you can get prime cuts of meat, organic vegetables, and fragrant cheeses. If you want a more structured meal, this is generally a pretty good neighborhood to find a deal, as prices are lower than in the city center.

👍 Pie Minister

PIES $

Gabriel's Wharf, 56 Upper Ground

☎020 7928 5755; www.pieminister.co.uk

Gabriel's Wharf is a little square by the river ringed with cafes and restaurants, of which Pie Minister is by far the best. Their pies are creative twists on classic British dishes; there's steak and kidney, plus the Matador Pie (chorizo, tomatoes, and sherry) and the Thai Chook Pie (chicken green curry). Vegetarians, rejoice! Forget the perennial roasted vegetables option in favor of pies like the Heidi (sweet potato and goat cheese). Round off your all-pie meal with a dessert pie. The store is tiny, so there's no place to sit in winter, but in summer there's plenty of seating on the patio.

▶ ⇄ ⊖Waterloo. Walk toward the main roundabout and onto Waterloo Rd., then turn right onto Upper Ground. $ Pies £4.25; with gravy, mashed potatoes, and mushy peas £5.95. ⏰ Open daily 10am-5pm.

Tsuru

JAPANESE $

4 Canvey St.

☎020 7928 2228; www.tsuru-sushi.co.uk

This simple and efficient sushi spot is the perfect place to grab lunch if you're at the Tate Modern. The sushi comes packaged in containers suspiciously reminiscent of the stuff they serve at Tesco, but it's all freshly made by the chefs, whom you can watch working while you eat. In addition to various sushi combinations, you can order their fabulous *katsu* curry or *katsu bento,* slices of meat or vegetables fried and served on a mound of rice with tasty sauces. Tsuru offers all the ease of a fast-food restaurant with the flavor (and sake!) of a proper Japanese joint.

▶ ⇄ ⊖Southwark. Walk down Blackfriars Rd. toward the river, turn right onto Southwark Rd., and left onto Canvey St. $ Sushi boxes £4-6. Katsu £6. ⏰ Open M-F 11am-9pm, Sa noon-7pm.

SOUTH KENSINGTON AND CHELSEA

Most restaurants in these neighborhoods cater to the rich and powerful, but there's also a good selection of delicious mid-range eateries, and the main roads (King's Rd., Old Brompton Rd., High St. Kensington) are packed with more inexpensive options.

🏆 Buona Sera

ITALIAN $$

289A King's Rd.

☎020 7352 8827

If the bunk beds in your hostel haven't made you hate ladders, come to Buona Sera for good eats and even better interior design. The small restaurant manages to fit 14 tables into a tight space by stacking booths on top of each other. It's sort of like Tetris, except with delicious, affordable Italian food.

▶ ⇄ ⊖Sloane Sq. Exit the Tube and head straight down Sloane Sq. Turn onto King's Rd, which slants gently off to the left. Alternatively, take bus #11, 19, 22, 211, or 319. $ Salads £5. Pasta and risotto £9. Meat and fish main courses £14. ⏰ Open M-F noon-3pm and 6pm-midnight, Sa-Su noon-midnight.

Bumpkin
BRITISH $$$

109 Brompton Rd.

☎020 7341 0802; www.bumpkinuk.com

Every single thing in this restaurant, except for the olive oil (and we hope the wine) is British. The menu changes daily to accommodate the sustainable, seasonal organic ingredients. If this kind of eco-conscious ethos usually sends you running for the hills, read on—this is just plain ol' British food, done right. Dishes include pork chops with apple chutney, Scottish sea bass filet with pearl barley, and baked macaroni with local cheddar. Leave with your belly full and your carbon footprint light.

▶ ⇞ ⊖South Kensington. Exit down Old Brompton Rd. $ Appetizers £5.50-9. Main courses £12-20. ⏰ Open daily 11am-11pm.

Borscht 'n' Tears
RUSSIAN $$$

46 Beauchamp Pl.

☎020 7589 5003

Longing for Mother Russia? All the capitalism in South Ken getting you down? Never fear, comrade, this Eastern European enclave has enough vodka to fortify the entire Red Army. Enjoy comfort food just like your *babushka* used to make—dumplings, stroganoff, Chicken Kiev, and yes, borscht. Frequent live music gets the party started, and by the time you leave, you'll be feeling positively Slavic. Indulge your inner Soviet. You know you can't resist.

▶ ⇞ ⊖Knightsbridge. Turn left down Brompton Rd. and left onto Beauchamp Pl. $ Main courses £12-16. ⏰ Open daily 11am-1am.

Thai Square
THAI $$

19 Exhibition Rd.

☎020 7584 8359; www.thaisquare.net

Thai Square is a solid option for all the usual Thai favorites—spring rolls, curries, noodle dishes—in generous portions and with authentic flavors. One of the calmer restaurants in the museum area, Thai Square's serenity is aided by dark wooden furniture and delicate floral trimmings.

▶ ⇞ ⊖South Kensington. Turn right onto Thurloe St. and left onto Exhibition Rd. $ Appetizers £3-5. Main courses £7-12. ⏰ Open M-Sa noon-3pm and 6-11pm, Su noon-3pm and 6-10pm.

The Marketplace
EUROPEAN $$$

125 Sydney St.

☎020 7352 5600; www.marketplacerest.com

Befitting a restaurant located in the Chelsea Farmer's Market,

The Marketplace boasts a menu of fresh ingredients and a swath of picnic tables to eat it all on. Heaters keep the place bearable in winter, but if you must sit indoors you'll be welcomed by a similarly bright, farmhouse feel. This is Chelsea, so you're paying quite a bit more than you would back on the ranch, but the food—hummus, pesto linguine, steak, smoked salmon salad, etc.—is tasty and the mood is unfussy. That's a lot more than can be said for many of the neighbors.

▶ ⚐ ⊖Sloane Sq. Walk down King's Rd. and turn right onto Sydney St. Ⓢ Main courses £12-20. ⏰ Open daily 9am-8pm.

Pasha   MOROCCAN $$
1 Gloucester Rd.

☎020 7589 7969; www.pasha-restaurant.co.uk

It's not just the food that's exotic here. The whole restaurant is decked out with low tables, bejeweled curtains, and ornate lamps. Once you're done gawking at your surroundings, choose from a variety of North African delights like lamb tagine, *merguez* couscous, and saffron-stuffed zucchini.

▶ ⚐ ⊖Gloucester Rd. Turn left when leaving the station. Ⓢ Main courses £14-20. ⏰ Open M-W noon-12:30am, Th-Sa noon-1:30am, Su noon-12:30am.

The Orangery   CAFE $$$
Kensington Palace Gardens

☎020 7376 0239

Just across the lawn from Kensington Palace, the Orangery is the place to come to have tea and feel like a princess. The tea menus come with a selection of finger sandwiches, pastries, scones, and even a glass of Champagne. They serve other lunch options too, but who could resist the traditional afternoon tea in this proper English setting? Take it in the grand hall or on the patio outside, and remember to raise your pinky.

▶ ⚐ ⊖High St. Kensington. Turn right down Kensington High St. and head through the park and toward Kensington Palace. The Orangery is on the far side. Ⓢ Tea menus £15-33. ⏰ Open daily Mar-Sept 10am-6pm; Oct-Feb 10am-5pm.

My Old Dutch Pancake House   DUTCH $$
221 King's Rd.

☎020 7376 5650; www.myolddutch.com

The name says it all: this place dishes out delicious Dutch-style pancakes (i.e., crepes). Pick a savory filling, like smoked duck and spring onions or mozzarella and tomato, or go the sweeter route with lemon and sugar or banana, nuts, and chocolate sauce. Or, let's be honest, just get one of each. Top it all off with your favorite from their selection of Dutch beers.

▶ # ⊖Sloane Sq. Exit the Tube and go straight down Sloane Sq. The street slanting gently left is King's Rd. $ Savory crepes £8-11, sweet £5.50-8. ⏰ Open M-Sa 10:30am-10:45pm, Su 10:30am-10pm.

HYDE PARK TO NOTTING HILL

Queensway is lined with cheap Chinese, Indian, and Lebanese restaurants, so it's always a surefire place to find a decent and inexpensive, if generic, meal. Notting Hill Gate is packed with chain cafes and little else. Paddington is something of a mix between the two. Portobello Rd. has some quirky and interesting spots, while Westbourne Terrace has quite a few high-quality yet mid-price places mixed in with some exorbitantly expensive ones.

🍴 Otto — PIZZA $

6 Chepstow Rd.

☎020 7792 4088; www.ottopizza.co.uk

Cornmeal-crust pizza? Sounds exactly like the kind of soggy, bland culinary idea Britain is famous for (sorry, Jamie Oliver). But the pizzas at Otto are good enough to make even Italian food purists ask for seconds. The crusts are crisp and hearty, and the fillings are packed on—choose from options like fennel sausage and caramelized onion, or roasted eggplant and bleu cheese. The staff are very encouraging about experimentation, so you can either get a couple of slices to try or go for the chef's taster: a whole pizza where each slice is a different flavor.

▶ # ⊖Notting Hill Gate. Make a right down Pembridge Rd., which will turn into Pembridge Villas, and then a left onto Chepstow Rd. *i* Takeaway available. Gluten-free and vegetarian options always available. $ Slices £3.50; whole pizza (serves 2-3) £18. ⏰ Open M-F 5:30-11pm, Sa noon-11pm, Su noon-10pm.

🍴 Durbar Restaurant — INDIAN $

24 Hereford Rd.

☎020 7727 1947; www.durbartandoori.co.uk

It's hard to resist the warm smells from the kitchen of Durbar, where the same family has served up Indian specialties for the last 54 years. This was a popular Indian restaurant before Indian restaurants were popular, and—in a city brimming with Indian food—it still manages to be one of the best values. The menu ranges across India, with a collection of favorites and some unexpected dishes.

▶ 🪧 ⊖Bayswater. Left onto Queensway, left onto Moscow Rd., right onto Hereford toward Westbourne Grove. $ Starters £2-5. Main courses £6-9. Lunch special £4.50. ⏰ Open M-Th noon-2:30pm and 5:30-11:30pm, F 5:30-11:30pm, Sa-Su noon-2:30pm and 5:30-11:30pm.

La Bottega del Gelato

GELATO $

127 Bayswater Rd.

☎020 7243 2443

La Bottega Del Gelato, deservedly popular, schools the rest of the London ice cream scene with a variety of delicious homemade flavors. Enjoy it outside on Bayswater Rd. in their seating area or across the road in Hyde Park. Even in the heart of the city, this gelato will make you feel like you're on a quiet street in Roma. The Ferrero Rocher is especially good.

▶ 🪧 ⊖Bayswater. Right onto Queensway, follow it until you hit Bayswater Rd. ℹ Free Wi-Fi. $ 1 scoop £2; 2 scoops £3.50; 3 scoops £4.50. Milkshakes £3.50. ⏰ Hours change depending on the weather, but the store opens daily at 10:30am.

Charlie's Portobello Road Cafe

CAFE $

59A Portobello Rd.

☎020 7221 2422; www.charliesportobelloroadcafe.co.uk

Tucked away in a small alcove off busy Portobello Rd., Charlie's Portobello Road Cafe is a hidden gem in one of London's most trafficked areas. Despite serving classically British sandwiches like ham, cheddar, and chutney, Charlie's has a decidedly continental vibe, with large French windows and rustically worn wood tables. Main courses, salads, soups, and plenty of baked goods are also available.

▶ 🪧 ⊖Notting Hill Gate. Take a right onto Pembridge Rd. and then a left onto Portobello Rd. ℹ Free Wi-Fi. $ Sandwiches £4-6. Salads £6-8. Full English breakfast £9.50. ⏰ Open M-Sa 9am5pm, Su noon-3pm.

Tiny Robot

ITALIAN $$

78 Westbourne Grove

☎020 7065 6814; www.tnyrbt.com

This is the sort of kitschy diner/foodie establishment that only hipsters love, but the food is tasty and the decorations are simple (lots of exposed brick, pastel tiles, and chrome). Dining options vary from American bar classics like sliders to sophisticated Italian options like *cotechino* sausage, *arancini,* and *burrata.* At night, the bar serves elegant cocktails, but bites from the menu are available until late. On weekends, brunch is served.

▶ ⇞ ⊖Bayswater. Make a left onto Queensway and then a left onto Westbourne Grove. [$] Small dishes £2-6. Main courses £6-14. ⏰ Open M-Tu 5pm-midnight, W-F 5pm-2am, Sa 10am-2am, Su 10am-10:30pm.

MARYLEBONE AND BLOOMSBURY

The back streets of Bloomsbury offer some cheap ethnic restaurants and cafes where you can grab a meal that, if not particularly exciting for any culinary reason, will be unlikely to put you back more than 10 quid. Toward Marylebone, the main roads have a surplus of the usual chain restaurants, while Goodge St. has a smattering of more unique and flavorful (though a bit pricier) establishments.

🍴 La Fromagerie CHEESE $

2-6 Moxon St.

☎020 7935 0341; www.lafromagerie.co.uk

Cheese. Hundreds of different kinds of cheese, as far as the eye can see. If this thought delights and excites you, you'll enjoy La Fromagerie, a store that has its very own Cheese Room. Buffalo, goat, cow, sheep, soft, semi-soft, hard... they've got them all. Man cannot live on cheese alone, though (trust us, we've tried), so the store also stocks other gourmet goodies and a rustic cafe where you can get a sandwich, salad, or tart (and try some of the cheeses).

▶ ⇞ ⊖Baker St. Turn left onto Marylebone Rd., right onto Marylebone High St., and right again onto Moxon St. [$] Cheese prices vary wildly. Sandwiches £6. Salads £8 or £16 per kg. Picnic basket for 2 £30. ⏰ Open M-F 8am-7:30pm, Sa 9am-7pm, Su 10am-6pm.

🍴 Newman Arms BRITISH PIES $$

23 Rathbone St.

☎020 7636 1127; www.newmanarms.co.uk

Established in 1730, the Newman Arms has been serving succulent British pies about as long as the Queen's relatives have been on the throne. The menu reads like an ode to comfort food, with pies like beef and Guinness, steak and kidney, and lamb and rosemary. The exceedingly English upstairs dining room fills up fast, so be sure to reserve a table a day in advance during the summer and much further in advance during the winter (sometimes even months). Don't forget to save room for the gooey desserts as well.

► ⊖Goodge St. Turn left onto Tottenham Court Rd., left onto Tottenham St., left onto Charlotte St., and right onto Rathbone St. Enter through the corridor next to the entrance to the pub. $ Pies £10. Desserts £4.50. ⏰ Open M-F noon-3pm and 6-10pm.

Shibuya

JAPANESE $$

2 Acton St.

☎020 7278 3447

Shibuya is a no-fuss Japanese restaurant that strives to use locally sourced and sustainable ingredients. They serve freshly made sushi, but there are plenty of noodle and curry dishes available. The lunch specials are excellent deals (we like the filling vegetable tempura udon soup served with a salmon avocado sushi roll). Given how exorbitantly expensive fresh sushi tends to be in London, this place is a steal. The Zen-like room with delicate blossom wallpaper will only add to your peace of mind.

► ⊖King's Cross St. Pancras. Make a left leaving the station, stay on Euston as it turns into Pentonville Rd., then make a right onto King's Cross Rd. The restaurant is on the corner with Acton St. $ Sushi from £2.50. Main courses £7-10. Lunch specials £7.50.

Fairuz

LEBANESE $$

3 Blandford St.

☎020 7486 8108; www.fairuz.uk.com

This popular Lebanese spot is a solid neighborhood choice if you want a tasty sit-down meal without shelling out too much cash. Lamb features prominently on the menu; grilled or minced, it's always flavored with exotic spices. Starters include favorites like hummus and *baba ghanoush*. In the summer months, outdoor seating is available.

► ⊖Bond St. Left on Oxford St., and right onto James St., which will eventually turn into Thayer St. then make a right onto Blandford St. *i* Takeaway available. $ Starters £4-6. Main courses £12-17. ⏰ Open M-Sa noon-11pm, Su noon-10:30pm.

Gourmet Glossary

One of the best parts about going to London is not needing to learn another language. You should be able to understand your waiter—most of the time. But you might want to stash this list under the table in case you run into a phrase you don't recognize:

- **BANGERS** are sausages.
- **BLACK PUDDING** is sausage made from pig's blood and fat.
- **BROWN SAUCE** usually refers to HP sauce, which is made of malt vinegar, tamarind, tomatoes, and dates.
- **BUBBLE AND SQUEAK** means leftover vegetables and potatoes mashed together.
- **BUCKS FIZZ** is a mimosa.
- **FAIRY CAKES** are cupcakes. Fairies are too small to eat whole cakes.
- **JELLY** actually means jello. It's alive!
- **KIPPER** is smoked herring.
- **MASH** means mashed potatoes (most often in "bangers and mash").
- **OFFAL** refers to animal organs and entrails, usually liver and kidney meat.
- **RASHERS** are slices of bacon.
- **PUDDING** refers to all desserts, not just the kind you eat after having your wisdom teeth removed.
- **SOLDIERS** are small pieces of toast.
- **SPOTTED DICK** is a dessert with dried fruit or custard—not any other kind of dick.

Alara   ORGANIC, VEGETARIAN $

58-60 Marchmont St.

☎020 7837 1172; www.alarashop.com

If you're feeling a little overwhelmed by all the pints and pies that London has thrust upon you, come to this health-food store and cafe to cleanse your palate and your conscience. You can pick up all kinds of vegan, organic, or just generally hippie-ish groceries in the shop, while the cafe offers smoothies, frozen yogurt, and a delicious lunch buffet. The dishes are all vegetarian and include moussaka, spinach tortillas, and some magical things made from legumes. Seating is available on a sidewalk patio.

▶ ⇆ ⊖Russell Sq. Veer right when exiting the station and head up Marchmont St. [$] Smoothies and frozen yogurt £2-4. Buffet £1.15 per 100g. ⏰ Open M-F 8am-8pm, Sa 10am-6pm, Su 11am-6pm. Buffet available until about 4pm.

NORTH LONDON

👍 La Crêperie de Hampstead — CREPERIE, STREET STAND $

Around 77 Hampstead High St.
www.hampsteadcreperie.com

Walking down Hampstead High St. from the underground station, you may notice people ravenously eating crepes out of small conical cups. Walk a bit farther and you'll come upon La Crêperie de Hampstead, which has been serving the city's best crepes for over 30 years. The crepes are expertly crafted—a perfect balance of light and doughy—and the ingredients, sweet or savory, are bursting with flavor.

▶ ⇆ ⊖Hampstead. Turn left onto Hampstead High St. ℹ No seating. [$] Sweet crepes £3.40-3.90; savory £4.30-4.80. ⏰ Open M-Th 11:45am-11pm, F-Su 11:45am-11:30pm.

👍 Le Mercury — FRENCH $$

140A Upper St.
☎020 7354 4088; www.lemercury.co.uk

Le Mercury proves that good French food doesn't have to be expensive. Most starters are under £4, and all main courses are under £8. These include dishes as luxurious as *ballotine de foie gras,* lobster ravioli, and pork belly with *celeriac confit.* Enjoy them in the yellow interior by flickering candlelight and you may wonder why they even bothered building the Chunnel.

▶ ⇆ ⊖Angel. Exit and turn right onto Upper St. [$] Starters £4. Main courses £8. Desserts £3. ⏰ Open M-Sa noon-1am, Su noon-11:30pm.

Mango Room — CARIBBEAN $$

10-12 Kentish Town Rd.
☎020 7482 5065; www.mangoroom.co.uk

Mango Room offers a pleasant escape from the bustle of nearby Camden Town. The bright paintings, reggae, and delicious

Caribbean dishes—like ackee and saltfish, jerk chicken, and curries—will cheer you up on a rainy London afternoon.

▶ 🪧 ⊖Camden High St. Turn left onto Camden High St., left onto Camden Rd., and left onto Kentish Town Rd. [$] Lunch main courses £7-8.50. Dinner main courses £10.50-11. Happy hour cocktails £4. ⏰ Open M-Th noon-11pm, F-Sa noon-1am, Su noon-11pm. Kitchen open daily noon-11pm. Happy hour 6-8pm.

Gallipoli
TURKISH $$

102 Upper St.

☎020 7359 0630; www.cafegallipoli.com

Bronze lamps, painted plates, and wooden knick-knacks make this restaurant feel like a Turkish bazaar. The food—tangy feta, smoky grilled meats, and delicately spiced pilafs—feels no less authentic. Choose from a selection of mezze, or order a more traditional main course.

▶ 🪧 ⊖Angel. Turn right onto Upper St. [$] Mezze £3-5. Main courses £8-12. ⏰ Open M-Th 11am-11pm, F 11am-midnight, Sa 10am-midnight, Su 10am-11pm.

InSpiral Cafe
VEGAN, CAFE $$

250 Camden High St.

☎020 7428 5875; www.inspiralled.net

A stupendous view over Camden Lock accompanies Inspiral Cafe's great selection of vegan food. You can choose between curries, lasagnas, breakfast scrambles, and even chocolate truffles.

▶ 🪧 ⊖Camden Town. Turn right onto Camden High St. ℹ Free Wi-Fi. [$] Breakfast £3-5. Main courses £7-10. ⏰ Open M-Th 8am-10pm, F 8am-2am, Sa 9am-2am, Su 9am-11:30pm.

EAST LONDON

Most of East London's culinary offerings are packed into the unbeatable **Brick Lane.** If you're looking for curry, you'd have to be blind (not to mention smell-challenged) to miss it. There are other ethnic restaurants of various stripes, as well as the requisite number of cafes for an area this rife with flannel and skinny jeans.

👍 Cafe 1001
CAFE $

91 Brick Ln.

☎020 7247 9679; www.cafe1001.co.uk

Hip East Enders bask in the British sun's occasional appearances while chatting over coffee from Cafe 1001's year-round outdoor cart. But they serve more than just coffee—the barbeque also grills all sorts of affordable burgers. Inside, patrons kick back in the warehouse-like space, where a variety of sandwiches and light food are served against a backdrop of Brazilian jams. At night, the salad bar turns into a real bar, and the back room becomes a venue for up-and-coming bands and DJs. Bloc Party filmed their video for "The Prayer" here. "East London is a vampire," as the boys would say.

▶ 🪧 🚇Aldgate East. Turn left onto Whitechapel Rd., left onto Osborn St., then continue onto Brick Ln. ℹ Live bands on Tu (rock) and W (folk and jazz). Swing dancing classes Th 11am-5pm. Club night F-Su 7pm-midnight. Free Wi-Fi. $ Cover £3-5 after midnight. Burger and chips £5. Coffee £1.20-2. Credit card min. £4. ⏰ Open daily 7am-midnight, often stays open all night F-Su.

Mien Tay — VIETNAMESE $

122 Kingsland Rd.

☎020 7729 3074; www.mientay.co.uk

What Brick Lane is to Bengali food, this stretch of Kingsland Rd. is to Vietnamese. Mien Tay sets itself above the rest with low prices and high-quality crispy spring rolls, fragrant *pho,* and tasty noodle dishes (try the lemongrass and curry noodles). The service is swift and the dining room is bright and roomy.

▶ 🪧 🚇Hoxton. Make a left after leaving the station, then a right onto Cremer St., and a left onto Kingsland Rd. $ Starters £2-5. Main courses £5-9. ⏰ Open M-Th noon-11pm, F-Sa noon-11:30pm, Su noon-11pm.

SOUTH LONDON

👍 Franco Manca — PIZZERIA $

Unit 4, Market Row

☎020 7738 3021; www.francomanca.co.uk

You'd be forgiven for thinking that you've stumbled through a wormhole to Naples when you step into this tiny pizzeria behind the Brixton Tube station. The chefs chatter away in Italian as they flip dough and transform it into one of the six gourmet pizzas on their seasonal menu. Besides the standard, perfectly crisped margherita, you can try pies with toppings like chorizo, organic pecorino cheese, and wild broccolini. Each individual pizza comfortably serves one, and you can wash it down with something from their well-curated selection of beer and wine.

▶ ✦ ⊖Brixton. Make a left leaving the Tube, a quick left onto Electric Ave., then a right onto Electric Ln. and a left onto Market Row. Ⓢ Pizzas £4.50-7. ⓧ Open M-Sa noon-5pm.

▨ Negril   CARIBBEAN $$

132 Brixton Hill
☎020 8674 8798

Brixton is famous for its Afro-Caribbean food, and Negril is the place to sample some of the best of it. You can try regional special-ties like callaloo (a leafy green), saltfish fritters, and goat curry, or go with something more familiar, like roasted chicken or barbeque ribs. Negril's rich, spicy gravy might be the best we've ever tasted. They also have quite a few vegan options, based on the traditional Rastafarian diet. Their weekend brunch is very popular.

▶ ✦ ⊖Brixton. Make a left leaving the Tube and continue as the road be-comes Brixton Hill. *i* Delivery and takeaway available. No alcohol served, but you can BYOB for a £2.50 corkage charge per person. Ⓢ Main courses £7-12. ⓧ Open M-F 5-10pm, Sa-Su 10am-10pm.

The Common   CAFE $

21 The Pavement
☎020 7622 4944

The Common is a simple French-style cafe across from Clapham Common with some of the cheapest prices in the area. You can grab sandwiches to picnic in the park, or hang out on one of the two levels of seating. At night, they serve bistro-style dishes (steak, pasta, etc.), but they're better known for their abundant breakfast, which includes everything from granola with yogurt and fresh fruit to a full English fry-up.

▶ ✦ ⊖Clapham Common. Go left from the station and continue along The Pavement toward the park. Ⓢ Sandwiches £2-4.50. Brunch and breakfast dishes £4-7. Main courses £7-12. ⓧ Open daily 7am-10pm.

WEST LONDON

▨ Sufi   PERSIAN $$

70 Askew Rd.
☎020 8834 4888; www.sufirestaurant.com

A very unassuming corner of West London hides this very unassuming restaurant with what many people swear is the best Persian food in London. It's easy to pass by the nonde-script storefront, unless the window plastered with stickers and reviews happens to catch your eye. Inside the elegant dining room, you'll find perfectly charcoal-grilled skewers of meat, exotic stews, and hearty noodle soups, all for very reasonable prices—you can easily get a full meal here for £8.

▶ ⛙ ⊖Shepherd's Bush Market. Make a right down Uxbridge Rd. when leaving the station, then after about 15min. make a left down Askew Rd. You can also take Bus #207 to the beginning of Askew Rd. $ Starters £2-4. Main courses £7-12. ⏰ Open M-Sa noon-11pm, Su noon-10:30pm.

Patio

POLISH $$

5 Goldhawk Rd.

☎020 8743 5194

You may not always have been raring to try Polish cuisine, but this restaurant will make you realize what you've been missing. Owned by a former Polish opera singer, Patio is filled with warm carpets and over-stuffed chairs, meant to create a casual but pleasant (read: comforting and grandmotherly) atmosphere. Diners enjoy traditional Polish fare like stuffed pancakes, veal, and cucumber and dill salad. The portions are hearty—even one of the "lighter" dishes can serve as a full meal. There's even a dusty-sounding piano for guests to bang out a tune.

▶ ⛙ ⊖Shepherd's Bush. Cross Uxbridge Rd. and turn right onto Shepherd's Bush Green. Follow it until it becomes Goldhawk Rd. $ Main courses £8-13. 3-course meal £15. ⏰ Open M-F noon-3pm and 5-11pm, Sa-Su 6-11:30pm.

Nightlife

Pubs are the fabric of British life; most are open daily 11am to 11pm. The best ones claim residence in the oldest drinking locations in London, meaning that people have been drunk there since the dawn of time. Be wary of the "George Orwell drank here" line—you'll see those claims everywhere, because not only were many British icons fantastic drunks, they were also prolific walkers.

"But," you say, "how can it be nightlife if it closes down at 11pm?" Good question. If you seek the club scene of say, Barcelona, go to Barcelona. London is less lively than many European cities, and the elitist impulse often rears its head in British club life (especially in South Kensington and Chelsea, where many clubs are "members only"). The West End is full of bar-club hybrids that fill with cocktail-drinkers after work and morph into dance clubs on the weekends. This is also the only neighborhood where you're guaranteed to find something open after midnight on a Monday. Shoreditch is London's other nightlife center, and, though it's less prolific during the week, you'll find better music, cheaper prices, and more plaid than high heels. Speakeasy-style bars focusing on mixology and feeling hip can be found throughout the city. Keep an eye on local listings (in free daily newspapers, posters, and flyers) to find out what's going on after dark.

THE CITY OF LONDON

Pricey pubs filled with business suits are a dime a dozen in the City, but your options improve as you head north toward **Clerkenwell.**

Fabric

CLUB

77A Charterhouse St.

☎020 7336 8898; www.fabriclondon.com

Despite being one of London's most famous clubs, Fabric has never lost its underground edge. Perhaps that's due to their carefully cultivated soundtrack—you won't hear David Guetta here, just cutting-edge dub, drum 'n bass, and techno. The space, a renovated warehouse full of deconstructed industrial decor, is the perfect place for the club's fun-loving clientele to dance. Look out for hidden quirks and flourishes, like 3D floor maps in the stairwells and a copy of Rubens's *Samson and Delilah* presiding over the smokers' courtyard. Or, entertain yourself by watching the guy with the dilated pupils try to figure out the faucets in the futuristic bathrooms (hint: there are buttons on the floor).

▶ ⛙ ⊖Farringdon. Turn left onto Cowcross St. and continue until you hit Charterhouse St. $ Cover F-Sa £15-20, students £10; Su £10/5. Get discounts by buying tickets in advance. Beer £4.50. ⏰ Open F 10pm-6am, Sa 11pm-8am, Su 11pm-6am.

The Jerusalem Tavern

PUB

55 Britton St.

☎020 7490 4281; www.stpetersbrewery.co.uk

The Jerusalem Tavern is the kind of London pub where you might be convinced you're back in the 18th century. The tavern is as bare as they come: a narrow, wooden interior without even any music playing. It's the only tavern in London to offer all of the St. Peter's ales. These specialized brews—including Golden Ale, Ruby Red Ale Honey Porter, and Cream Stout—are worth trying, though we're not saying you should try all of them at once... that would be irresponsible. Or so we hear.

▶ ⛙ ⊖Farringdon. Turn left onto Cowcross St., left onto Turnmill St., right onto Benjamin St., and left onto Britton St. $ Pints £3.25. ⏰ Open M-F 11am-11pm.

The Slaughtered Lamb

PUB

34-35 Great Sutton St.

☎020 7253 1516; www.theslaughteredlambpub.com

Don't be put off by this pub's macabre name—it comes from

this neighborhood's former career as London's meatpacking district. The Slaughtered Lamb feels a bit like a gigantic old living room with leather couches, comfy armchairs, and framed pictures around a fireplace (though most living rooms don't have this interesting a mix of indie rock and hip hop playing in the background). Downstairs, the music continues with frequent live shows and occasional comedy acts.

▶ ♯ ⊖Barbican. Turn left onto Goswell Rd. and left onto Great Sutton St. Ⓢ Pints from £3.60. Ⓣ Open M-Th 11:30am-midnight, F 11:30am-1am, Sa noon-1am, Su 12:30-10:30pm.

THE WEST END

For many people, the West End is synonymous with London nightlife. On the plus side, this is the one part of the city where you're guaranteed to find something to do at 1am on a Monday. But the price for that is a glut of overcrowded and expensive bars and clubs. The truly chic head to private clubs in fancier areas, so the dominant theme in the West End is bar-and-club combos where everyone's trying a little too hard. Don't despair, though. Soho has the highest concentration of GLBT nightlife in the city, and the neighborhood draws crowds looking to have a good time. Mixed in with the bad suits and tourist traps, you'll find one of London's best clubs and a few quality bars.

⚑ The Borderline   CLUB

Orange Yard, off Manette St.

☎020 7734 5547; venues.meanfiddler.com/borderline/home

In the sea of booty-shaking Top 40 that is the West End, The Borderline offers something completely different. Though the club is a bare, dark basement with the same drunken dancing as at any London club, here you'll be moving to the likes of Joy Division, the Smiths, The Kooks, and Vampire Weekend. The crowd is devoted to the music, and you can't help but get into the spirit of things when everyone shouts the lyrics to "Friday I'm in Love." The club also hosts live music (see **Arts and Culture**). Plus, where else in the West End can you get a beer for two quid? (Answer: nowhere.)

▶ ♯ ⊖Tottenham Court Rd. Turn right onto Charing Cross Rd. and right onto Manette St. ⓘ Focus on punk on W, Student Night on Th, indie rock and Brit pop on F-Sa. Ⓢ Cover W-Th £5; F-Sa £7. Frequent £2 drink specials. Ⓣ Open W-Sa 11pm-4am.

Dirty Martini

BAR, CLUB

11-12 Russell St.

☎0844 371 2550; www.dirtymartini.uk.com

This bar's martini creations—fruity, chocolatey, fizzy, and everything in between—are impressive enough. But it gets better: drinks are half price during happy hour. As it gets later, the stylish lounge transforms into a dance club. The drink prices may rise, but that's offset by the fact that this is one of the only clubs in the West End that never charges cover. To top it off, Dirty Martini offers something even rarer than a straight man at a Bieber concert: free coat check. So you can get two martinis. Just remember what Dorothy Parker said.

▶ 🚇 Covent Garden. Head down James St. to the Covent Garden Piazza, turn left and go around it until you come to the corner of Russell St. $ Beers £4. Cocktails £8-9. ⏰ Open M-W 5pm-1am, Th-Sa 5pm-3am, Su 5-11pm. Happy hour M-Th 5-10pm, F-Sa 5-8pm, Su 5-11pm.

Ain't Nothin' But...

BAR, LIVE MUSIC

20 Kingly St.

☎020 7287 0514; www.aintnothinbut.co.uk

Your woman done left you? Your baby got you down? Come commiserate (or drink away your sorrows) at this excellent blues bar, where there's live music every night of the week. From established bands to open-mic nights to jam sessions, they've got it all. Even when no one's performing, a contingent of grizzled regulars line the bar, nursing double bourbons and enjoying the CD collection.

▶ 🚇 Oxford Circus. Head down Regent St., turn right onto Great Marlborough St., and right onto Kingly St. $ Nominal cover charge F-Sa after 8:30pm. Beers from £3.50. Double bourbon £6.60. ⏰ Open M-Th 5pm-1am, F 5pm-2:30am, Sa 3pm-2:30am, Su 3pm-midnight.

Heaven

CLUB, GLBT

Under the Arches, Villiers St.

☎020 7930 2020; www.heavennightclub-london.com

This gigantic, multi-room club is home to a variety of popular GLBT and mixed nights. Mondays have "Popcorn," a student-friendly event with good drink specials and a welcoming door policy; the music varies from hip hop to techno to classic dance tunes. Thursday through Saturday the club is run by G-A-Y, London's biggest GLBT party organization. Friday night brings "Camp Attacks" (with amazingly cheesy disco music) and performances by famous pop stars. Saturdays are usually the most popular night at Heaven.

▶ Charing Cross. Turn right from the station and head down Villiers St. The club is under the archway about halfway down. $ Cover £4-5; usually free before midnight or if you sign up on the guest list. ⏰ Open M 11pm-6am, Th 11pm-3am, F-Sa 11pm-5am.

Freud

BAR

198 Shaftesbury Ave.

☎020 7240 9933

Freud, standing out with a laid-back, bohemian atmosphere, is the West End bar for those trying to pretend they're not in the West End. You won't hear any Beyoncé, but Freud is nowhere near as pretentious as some of the bars in Shoreditch. The drinks are big and strong, but be careful about what you order if you don't want to be psychoanalyzed: the Slippery Nipple and Harvey Wallbanger are crying out for the great man's intervention.

▶ Piccadilly Circus. Turn right onto Shaftesbury Ave. $ Beer £3.50. Cocktails £5.50-7.50. Credit card min. £10. ⏰ Open M-Th 11am-11pm, F-Sa 11am-1am, Su noon-10:30pm.

Village

BAR, GLBT

81 Wardour St.

☎020 7478 0530; www.village-soho.co.uk

Early in the evening, Village looks like just another after-work bar (except with slightly nicer suits on slightly better-looking men). As the night wears on, however, it gets more exciting with drag queens, karaoke (Tuesdays and Wednesdays), go-go boys (Saturdays), and more. The slightly carnival-esque decorations and tantalizing cocktail menu only add to the fun.

▶ Piccadilly Circus. Turn right onto Shaftesbury Ave. then left onto Wardour St. $ Cocktails £6-7. ⏰ Open M-Sa 4pm-1am, Su 4-11:30pm.

Candy Bar

BAR, CLUB, GLBT

4 Carlisle St.

☎020 7287 5041; www.candybarsoho.com

Candy Bar is London's premier—and certainly most popular—lesbian bar and club. Ladies flock to the pop-colored bar for drinks, pool, and dancing. Boys are allowed if they bring at least two female friends, but they're barred from the downstairs floor when dancers are performing. DJs spin records Wednesday through Sunday; the music varies from hip hop to chart hits to funk and soul. Check out the ridiculous Monday drink specials.

▶ Tottenham Court Rd. Turn left onto Oxford St., left onto Dean St., and right onto Carlisle St. $ Cover £5 F-Sa after 10pm. Drinks £1.50-6. ⏰ Open M-Th 5pm-3am, F-Sa 4pm-3am, Su 4pm-12:30am.

WESTMINSTER

Westminster isn't an ideal location for nightlife, pubs, or clubs. Enjoy it during the day, and then take the party elsewhere, old sport—unless you're in the market for really good beer.

Cask — BEER HEAVEN

6 Charlwood St.

☎020 7630 7225; www.caskpubandkitchen.com

Whether or not you know the difference between a dubbel and a tripel, or that gueuze is the weirdest beer you'll ever taste, Cask has a drink for you. Their beer "menu" is actually a binder full of hundreds upon hundreds of bottled beers from around the world. A couple dozen more are on tap, and they rotate the selection so they can accommodate as many rare and novel brews as possible. Despite being a true aficionado's bar, neophytes will also feel right at home; the staff is always ready to make recommendations, and refrain from snobbery when responding to even the most basic questions and silliest mispronunciations. Ample seating ensures that, despite the bar's popularity, you'll be able to enjoy your pint comfortably.

▶ Pimlico. Turn right onto Tachwood St., Cask is at the corner on the right with Charlwood St. *i* Free Wi-Fi (as if you needed an excuse to spend more time here). $ Pints start around £3.70, but vary wildly from there. ⏰ Open M 4-11pm, Tu-Su noon-11pm.

Brass Monkey — PUB

250 Vauxhall Bridge Rd.

☎020 7834 0553; www.brass-monkeybar.co.uk

Unless you're absolutely gasping for a pint the second you leave Victoria station, ignore the tourist trap pubs nearby and walk a few minutes to this significantly more appealing establishment. Brass Monkey has a modest selection of draft beers, two excellent cask ales, and a decent wine list, but the real draw is the atmosphere. It's tasteful and polished, with locals enjoying pints and conversation across its two floors.

▶ ✝ ⊖Victoria. Turn right onto Vauxhall Bridge Rd. Ⓢ Pints £3.65. 🕐 Open M-Sa 11am-11pm.

THE SOUTH BANK

Back in Shakespeare's day, the South Bank was a hotbed of taverns, brothels, and bear-baiting. Things have calmed down a bit since then, but this is still a great place to find a pint or a stiff drink. Plenty of spots are clustered around London Bridge and Borough.

◪ The Hide   BAR

39-45 Bermondsey St.

☎020 7403 6655; www.thehidebar.com

You automatically feel a few degrees classier when you step inside this relaxed cocktail bar, without even having to change out of the jeans you've been wearing for a week straight. The Hide has candlelight, plenty of space, leather couches, and crackly jazz—but also a totally unpretentious atmosphere, and a crowd that includes everyone from backpackers to young lovers to old men in suspenders. The focus is on the cocktail menu, with oodles of drinks carefully mixed from apothecary-like glass bottles. Try the Boston Tea Party, which serves two from a porcelain tea pot into tiny little cups.

▶ ✝ ⊖London Bridge. Walk toward the bridge and turn right onto Tooley St., then right onto Bermondsey St. Ⓢ Most spirits £4. Cocktails £7-8. 🕐 Open Tu 5pm-midnight, W-Th 5pm-1am, F-Sa 5pm-2am, Su 3-10:30pm.

Southwark Tavern   PUB

22 Southwark St.

☎020 7403 0257; www.thesouthwarktavern.co.uk

You can go on the gimmicky London Dungeon experience, or you can come here and drink in one of the subterranean cells on the pub's lower floor. This place used to be a prison (it seems like half of the South Bank was), and it retains its original brick-and-iron-bars style. Doing better than bread and water, the pub offers 21 beers on draft, including a number of American imports (Sierra Nevada, Brooklyn Lager) if you're feeling homesick.

▶ ✝ ⊖London Bridge. Exit down Borough High St. and the pub is where Southwark St. splits off. 𝑖 Quiz night on Tu. Ⓢ Pints £4. 🕐 Open M-W 11am-midnight, Th-F 11am-1am, Sa 10am-1am, Su noon-midnight.

London Skittles

While the majority of Londoners today associate skittles with candy, a few old-timers picture bowling. Imbibing ale instead of tasting the rainbow, participants in this traditional pub game hurl a 10 lb. *fromage*-shaped hunk of wood at a diamond of nine pins, aiming to clear the lane in the least amount of throws. Skittles has been played since Danish sailors brought it up the Thames in the 17th century. Nothing kills a good drinking game quite like a world war, but skittles has been making a comeback in the London drunken debauchery scene. Stop by the Freemasons Arms on Tuesdays 8-11pm or Saturdays 6-9pm for a game. (81-82 Long Acre ☎020 7836 3115 🚏 ⊖Covent Garden. ⏰ Open daily 11am-late.)

SOUTH KENSINGTON AND CHELSEA

🍺 The Drayton Arms — PUB

153 Old Brompton Rd.

☎020 7835 2301; www.thedraytonarmssw5.co.uk

The Drayton Arms is a comfortable, well-kept pub that mixes the classiness of its postcode (chandeliers, high ceilings) with laid-back ease (oversize couches, worn wooden tables). Enjoy a fine selection of beers around the fireplace, then see a play or film in the first floor's black-box theater, which features everything from improv comedy to classic foreign films.

▶ 🚏 ⊖Gloucester Rd. Turn right onto Gloucester Rd. and right onto Old Brompton Rd. $ Pints around £3.80. ⏰ Open M-F 11am-midnight, Sa-Su 10am-midnight.

🍺 The Troubadour Club — LIVE MUSIC, BAR

263-267 Old Brompton Rd.

☎020 7370 1434; www.troubadour.co.uk

Many famous acts have graced the Troubadour's small stage since its founding in 1954. The hanging string lights have illuminated the likes of **Bob Dylan, Jimi Hendrix,** and **Joni Mitchell,** and pictures of these artists cover the tabletops. To this day, The Troubadour is a community of aspiring and acclaimed artists bound together by the intoxicating atmosphere of good drinks and great music. Come here to see some of the city's most exciting acts before they make it big.

▶ Gloucester Rd. Turn right onto Gloucester Rd., then turn right onto Old Brompton Rd. *i* Live music most nights. Poetry night every other M. Friday shows 21+. $ Cover usually £5-10; cash only. ⏰ Open M-W 8pm-midnight, Th-Sa 8pm-2am, Su 8pm-midnight. Happy hour Tu-Su 8-9pm.

Miss Q's — CLUB, BAR

180-184 Earl's Court Rd.
☎020 7370 5358; www.missqs.com

This old-school rock 'n' roll bar and club provides enough kitschy Americana to satisfy those still sad they missed the Elvis era. There's diner food on the menu, three classic pool tables, red lights, and black leather. Wednesday has live music, mostly rock and blues, while Thursday through Saturday nights host DJs diverging slightly from the theme by playing a range from classic soul to the latest hip hop. It may feel a bit schizophrenic, but it certainly gets people moving on the dance floor.

▶ Earl's Court. Turn left when exiting the station. $ Cover Th-F £5 after 10pm; Sa £5 after 9pm. Pints £4. Cocktails £7-11. ⏰ Open M-W 5pm-midnight, F-Sa 5pm-2am, Su 5pm-midnight. Happy hour M-Th 5-8pm.

The Blackbird — PUB

209 Earl's Court Rd.
☎020 7835 1855

The Blackbird is the quintessential local pub, with a long bar, plenty of booths, and unassuming rock playing softly overhead. It also serves many varieties of the Fuller's brand of (wholesomely British) beer. The food is the usual pies and Sunday roasts. At the edge of Kensington, it's less expensive and more authentic than the other "local English pubs" to the east.

▶ Earl's Court. Just across the road from the station, slightly to the right. $ Pints from £3.50. ⏰ Open M-Sa 11am-11pm, Su 11am-10:30pm.

Janet's Bar — BAR

30 Old Brompton Rd.
☎020 7581 3160

Janet's is the closest thing to a dive bar that you'll find in South Kensington. The walls are plastered with photos of regulars and Red Sox and Yankees pennants (closer together than most fans would like). It's still popular with the locals, despite the Americana—there are even rumors of occasional celebrity sightings. If the atmosphere doesn't make you feel welcome, the Beatles sing-alongs will, and it's one of the few bars in the neighborhood open past 11pm.

▶ ♯ ⊖South Kensington. As you exit the station, Old Brompton Rd. is across the street. *i* Live music Tu-Su after 9:30pm. Ⓢ Beer around £4.50. Cocktails £6.50-8.50. Credit card min. £3. ⏰ Open M-W 11:45am-1am, Th 11:45am-1:30am, F 11:45am-2:30am, Sa noon-2:30am, Su 2pm-1am.

HYDE PARK TO NOTTING HILL

For all the bustle around Bayswater during the day, it's pretty deserted at night. Notting Hill is largely residential, and the few nightlife spots it does have are dominated by businesspeople grabbing drinks on their way home from work. However, Portobello Rd. has a sprinkling of good bars that pop up when the shops close, although the long street can feel even longer and more desolate at night.

▨ Notting Hill Arts Club   CLUB

21 Notting Hill Gate

☎020 7460 4459; www.nottinghillartsclub.com

Notting Hill is not a place that makes you think of exuberant dancing, cutting-edge music, and cheap covers. And yet, tucked underground just off the main road lies this exciting den offering all those things and more. One room contains a circular bar with tables and couches set into the wall for lounging; the other has the dance floor and stage. There are virtually no decorations to speak of, so nothing will distract from your gyrations. Each night has a different mix of musical genres: Wednesday is indie and punk; Thursday has a supremely popular offering of hip hop and dub; Friday and Saturday might feature soul and funk, salsa, or who knows what else. The crowd varies from well-dressed young professionals to urban b-boy types who clearly know what this place is about.

▶ ♯ ⊖Notting Hill Gate. The door isn't well marked, but look for the smoking area and metal fences keeping the entrance line in place. *i* 18+; make sure to bring proof of age. Sign up for the guest list via Facebook for Th nights. Some special events pop up occasionally on other days. Ⓢ Cover varies, generally £5-8; free on W. Beer £3. Cocktails from £6. ⏰ Open W-Sa usually 8pm-2am.

▨ Portobello Star   BAR

171 Portobello Rd.

☎020 7229 8016; www.portobellostarbar.co.uk

We can't decide which we like best: the cheeky drink descriptions on the menu or the drinks themselves. Clearly at the forefront of the cocktail revolution, the libations at Portobello Star are creative and made from top-notch ingredients. The overall feeling of the place is that they take their booze (and not much else) seriously. You'll hear your favorite classic rock, indie hits, R and B, soul, and hip hop from the bar or the leather couches in the calmer chill-out room on the first floor. The crowd is in their early 20s to early 30s, clad in everything from dresses and heels to flannel and tattoos—or all four at once. During the day, the pub transforms into a cafe that serves pies made by the famous Ginger Pig butchers.

▶ Notting Hill Gate. Take a right onto Pembridge Rd. and then left onto Portobello Rd. $ Cocktails £7-10. ⏰ Open M-Th 10am-midnight, F-Sa 10am-1am, Su 10am-midnight.

Portobello Gold — PUB

95 Portobello Rd.

☎020 7229 8528; www.portobellogold.com

Portobello Gold is an old-fashioned pub with a crowd that sings along to the classic rock soundtrack. The clientele represents the whole age spectrum—from young hipsters to 70-something locals. Basically, there's a whole lot of plaid. They have a good selection of beers on tap, and a full-service restaurant with pub grub (and famous oysters) in the back. Especially popular on Saturdays after 11pm.

▶ Notting Hill Gate. Take right onto Pembridge Rd. and then left onto Portobello Rd. *i* Live music Su 6:30-10pm. $ ½ pints from £3.60. Wine £4-6. Cuban cigars £10. ⏰ Open M-Th 10am-noon, F-Sa 10am-12:30am, Su 10am-11:30pm.

MARYLEBONE AND BLOOMSBURY

While Bloomsbury is filled with universities, most students only live in the area for their first year (if at all). Student-oriented nightlife is thus limited to a few pubs here and there, while the rest of the area is dominated by the suits of the after-work crowd. However, a few old-fashioned haunts are worth checking out—perhaps more for sightseeing than nightlife purposes—and, since it's London, there's always a club or two to be found.

The Social — CLUB, BAR

5 Little Portland St.

☎020 7636 4992; www.thesocial.com

Though the upstairs, with its exposed light bulbs and bare

wood floor, looks like a typical hip bar, the underground space at the Social is where most of the action takes place. A ragingly popular hip-hop karaoke night takes place here every other Thursday, as well as club nights and live performances. Many nights have no cover charge. The Social is a lively contrast to the scores of traditional pubs filled with businessmen that surround the area and is the closest to a club you're likely to find around here.

▶ ♯ ⊖Oxford Circus. Right onto Regent St., right onto Little Portland St. *i* DJs on the ground fl. most nights. Ⓢ Pints around £3.70. Cocktails around £7. Cover £5-7 on club night. Student cards will get you discounts on most covered nights. Credit card min. £10. ☼ Open M 5pm-midnight, Tu-W noon-midnight, Th-F noon-1am, Sa 7pm-1am.

▨ Purl   BAR
50/54 Blandford St.
www.purl-london.co.uk

Designed to look like an old-school speakeasy, Purl would be gimmicky if the theme weren't pulled off so well. From the subterranean darkness to the bartenders' 1920s-style vests, everything is crafted to make Al Capone feel right at home. The crowd, though, tends to be very chic and modern. The drinks are pricey, but they are astounding works of art; some arrive steaming with liquid nitrogen, while others are packaged in a squat bottle complete with its own brown paper bag—and all are delicious and innovative mixtures, and definitely a far cry from a glass of bathtub gin.

▶ ♯ ⊖Bond St. Left onto Oxford St., and right onto James St., which will eventually turn into Thayer St. Right onto Blandford St. *i* Reservations recommended for tables; book online through their website. Ⓢ Cocktails £7.50-10. ☼ Open M-Th 5-11:30pm, F-Sa 5pm-midnight.

▨ The Golden Eagle   PUB
59 Marylebone Ln.
☎020 7935 3228

London is incredibly diverse, but sometimes you just want to experience something that feels truly British. So, what could be more perfect than hanging out with old men boozily belting out their favorite songs? Three nights a week at The Golden Eagle, the bespectacled Tony "Fingers" Pearson rolls out an old upright piano and proceeds to hammer out classics like "La Vie En Rose" and "Just One of Those Things." Between the alcohol-induced golden haze, the music, and the cheery staff, the pub is a living Capra film, and in no way is that a bad thing. Plus, the beer is cheap enough that soon you might be singing along with the crowd.

▸ 🚏 ⊖Bond St. Right onto Oxford St., left onto Marylebone Ln. *i* Music Tu and Th-F 8:30pm. $ Average pint £3.50. ⏰ Open M-Th 11am-11pm, F-Sa 11am-midnight, Su noon-7pm.

The Fitzroy Tavern PUB

16A Charlotte St.

☎020 7580 3714

Many pubs try to ensnare tourists by claiming they are the oldest pub in England or telling bizarre perversions of famous stories ("and that penny that Dickens gave to the little boy was spent on whiskey in our pub...") that lend a historical respectability to what is actually just a decrepit pub with bad ale. The Fitzroy Tavern actually has a published book about its history, with artifacts from that history coating its walls. Famous for the charitable program instated by the tavern to send kids on outings to the country and for the authors who frequented the pub—most notably **Dylan Thomas** and **George Orwell**—The Fitzroy Tavern is the real deal. Pints of the many tasty varieties of Sam Smith are cheap, the history's free, and there's a comedy night too.

▸ 🚏 ⊖Goodge St. Left onto Tottenham Ct. Rd., left on Tottenham St., left onto Charlotte St. *i* Comedy night W 8:30pm. $ Pints around £2.50. Credit card min. £10, plus 1.5% surcharge. ⏰ Open M-Sa noon-11pm, Su noon-10:30pm.

Scala CLUB

275 Pentonville Rd.

☎020 7833 2022; www.scala-london.co.uk

This multi-level club, just across the road from King's Cross, hosts a diversity of nighttime entertainment. From live bands to indie rock DJ mashups to hip hop to straight up club techno, there's always something loud playing. Scala is very popular with the younger end of the student crowd. Tickets are generally much cheaper in advance or with a flyer, so look online to plan ahead.

▸ 🚏 ⊖King's Cross St. Pancras. Head left when leaving the station. $ Cover varies, usually £5-12. ⏰ Opening hours depend on the event; club nights F-Sa 10pm-4am or later.

NORTH LONDON

Camden Town and the area around **Angel** come alive at night, but the scene is primarily limited to pubs and bars. Camden is also home to some important live-music venues.

▨ 69 Colebrooke Row   BAR

69 Colebrooke Row

☎07540 528 593; www.69colebrookerow.com

This lounge put a lot more effort into creating swanky atmosphere and inventive cocktail menu than they did their name. Of the cocktails, we like the Serafin (made with tequila, poire liqueur, and ginger beer) and the champagne topped with English rose aromatics. Popular among Islington yuppies and cocktail connoisseurs, the bar's vibe is saved from pretension by the impromptu ditties played by patrons on the upright piano.

▶ ♯ ⊖Angel. Turn right after leaving the station and stay to the right as you pass Islington Green. Then turn right onto Colebrooke Row. Ⓢ Cocktails £8.50. Ⓩ Open M-W 5pm-midnight, Th 5pm-1am, F-Sa 5pm-2am, Su 5pm-midnight.

Slim Jim's Liquor Store   BAR

112 Upper St.

☎020 7354 4364; www.slimjimsliquorstore.com

Not all American-themed establishments in London focus on hamburgers and BBQ; Slim Jim's pays homage in the form of old-school rockabilly and a sterling selection of bourbons. It's dark and divey, just like your favorite Delta honky-tonk. When the music gets going, couples show off their swing-dancing moves. Don't forget to appreciate the impressive collection of bras hanging from the ceiling, and feel free to add your own to the collection.

▶ ♯ ⊖Angel. Turn right and continue up Upper St. Ⓢ Bourbon and scotch £3-10. Pints from £3.75. Ⓩ Open M-W 4pm-2am, Th 4pm-3am, F-Sa noon-3am, Su noon-2am.

EAST LONDON

▨ The Book Club   BAR, CLUB

100 Leonard St.

☎020 7684 8618; www.wearetbc.com

No, this isn't a place where suburban housewives get together to discuss the latest Nicholas Sparks novel. In keeping with the ever-experimental, avant-garde atmosphere of East London, this multi-level former warehouse is a cafe, bar, lecture hall, dance club, art installation space, and more. During the week, there might be a Glam Poetry Slam or one of their signature "Thinking and Drinking" events—lectures on topics from laugh therapy to the connection between scent and memory. Thursday through Saturday are usually reserved for dancing. Thursdays are "Human Jukebox" (the crowd decides the music), while on Fridays and Saturdays they bring in excellent electronic and hip-hop DJs. The Book Club distills all the quirky creative energy of East London into one spot and adds a bar (or two).

▶ ⊖Shoreditch High St. Make a left after leaving the station, then a right onto Great Eastern St., and a left onto Leonard St. $ Cover varies from free to £12; on most F-Sa, it's £5 after 9pm. ⏰ Open M-W 8am-midnight, Th-F 8am-2am, Sa 10am-2am, Su 10am-midnight.

Strongroom Bar — BAR

120-124 Curtain Rd.

☎020 7426 5103; www.strongroombar.com

It seems like all the "cool" places in Shoreditch are down an alley or through a tunnel. Strongroom is no different, but it makes excellent use of its alleyway real estate with a large, heated patio area. Inside is a pub-like upper level and a downstairs lounge with couches and room for dancing. DJs spin old-school rock and soul, and there are occasionally live performances. They offer a truly stellar beer selection and some well-made cocktails.

▶ ⊖Shoreditch High St. Make a left after leaving the station, then a right onto Great Eastern St., and a right onto Curtain Rd. $ Pints from £3.50. ⏰ Open M 9am-11pm, Tu-W 9am-midnight, Th 9am-1am, F 9am-2am, Sa noon-2am, Su noon-10pm.

SOUTH LONDON

Brixton is teeming with pubs, clubs, and live-music venues. Most of them are clustered around the Tube station, so just wander about until you see something that strikes your fancy. Clapham's nightlife is popular with the yuppier crowd, who troll the cocktail bars up and down Clapham High St.

Hootenanny — BAR, CONCERT VENUE

95 Effra Rd.

☎020 7737 7273; www.hootenannybrixton.co.uk

The walk from the Tube takes you through a quiet residential neighborhood, but just as you start thinking you must have gone the wrong way, you come upon Hootenanny's warehouse-and-patio complex. Inside, you'll find a bar with pool tables and couches, plus the real draw of the venue: a concert space that hosts live roots, rock, reggae, and ska almost every night. Outside, there's a barbeque and smokers clustered around the many picnic tables. The cheerful vibe is infectious; it's hard not to groove along when an old Jamaican man is cutting a rug right next to you.

▶ ✝ ⊖Brixton. Make a left as you exit the station and continue on Effra Rd. as it forks off. *i* 21+. Ⓢ Most shows are free; occasional £5 cover. Beers from £3. 🕐 Hours vary, usually open W-Su 9am-2pm.

The White Horse   PUB
94 Brixton Hill
☎020 8678 6666; www.whitehorsebrixton.com

The White Horse is a large, laid-back pub with some curious touches—semi-pornographic bestial artwork, anyone?—that make it a bit more interesting than your average local. During the week, the pub attracts a young professional crowd for no-fuss drinks, while DJs liven things up on the weekends with hip hop, funk, and house. Sunday afternoons host live folk and jazz.

▶ ✝ ⊖Brixton. Make a left leaving the station and stay on the road as it turns into Brixton Hill. Ⓢ Pints from £3. 🕐 Open M-Th 5pm-midnight, F 4pm-3am, Sa noon-3am, Su noon-midnight.

WEST LONDON

▧ The Goldhawk   PUB
122-124 Goldhawk Rd.
☎020 8576 6921

The Goldhawk is just like that kid you know who is always ineffably cool without even trying—yeah, you know the one. Its indie-rock music is just a little bit better than the stuff played at other pubs. The beer selection is just a little bit more interesting—they've got an unusual Belgian brew or two mixed in with a wide selection of British ales. Its underdone-chic lounges and tables are just a little bit more artfully distressed. But, of course, it's totally unpretentious about the whole thing. This makes it one of the best simple hang-out-and-have-a-beer pubs in the city.

▶ ✝ ⊖Goldhawk Rd. Make a left when leaving the station. *i* Open-mic night

Th 8pm. Ⓢ Pints from £3.50. Frequent deals, like 4 beers for £10. ⏰ Open M-W noon-11pm, Th noon-midnight, F-Sa noon-12:30am, Su noon-11pm.

Dove   PUB

19 Upper Mall

☎020 8748 9474

This stretch of the Thames in Hammersmith feels calm, secluded, and rural, and any of the pubs along it are worthy of a visit. The Dove is probably the most beloved by locals. The taps hold a strong selection of British ales, and the kitchen serves up comforting pub grub. Best of all are the picnic tables, which let you sit right by the river in summer, and the toasty upper rooms, which provide a sheltered view in winter.

▶ ⚲ ⊖Ravenscourt Park. Make a left down Ravenscourt Rd., cross King St. onto Rivercourt Rd., and make a left onto Upper Mall. Ⓢ Pints from £3.50. ⏰ Open M-Sa 11am-11pm, Su noon-10:30pm.

Nightlife

Arts and Culture

From Shakespeare to the Sex Pistols, London has never been behind the times when it comes to the entertaining arts. Every time you take an escalator in a Tube station, the barrage of posters will remind you of the breadth and quality of the city's cultural opportunities. Experience the delights of the stage at a major West End musical, a quirky new production at the Young Vic, an elegant ballet at the Royal Opera House, or that famed British wit at one of the city's comedy clubs. If it's dulcet tones you're looking for, catch chamber music in St Martin-in-the-Fields, or check out an up-and-coming indie band at The Borderline. In the summer, the city explodes with festivals of all shapes and sizes. And for a city as expensive as London, cultural events can be surprisingly cheap. Whatever you need tickets for, make sure to check for deals—student discounts, standby tickets, and officially sanctioned theater passes can save you a lot of money.

Budget Arts and Culture

It's easy to shell out hundreds of pounds in London to see a West End production because "you're only in London once." The budget traveler is too smart to do this, though. Discounts, freebies, and the like reward all those who seek them in London—whether that be students, last-minute rushers, or just charming customers. This might sound obvious, but take the time to research these deals before buying tickets. Standby tickets at the Royal Opera House, 17th-century-style standing-room tickets at Shakespeare's Globe, and openly ticketed Olympics events like the marathon and triathlon will let you experience culture in London in a way that won't make your wallet angry.

THE 2012 OLYMPICS

As great as it always is to travel to London, 2012 is going to be special. Whether you're a sports buff, want to experience one of the world's greatest spectacles, or just dream of meeting Usain Bolt, being in London for the 30th Summer Olympics will be a remarkable experience. If you're going to be in the city between July 27 and August 12, read up on what you can expect to see.

Games Past and Present

HOSTESS WITH THE MOSTEST

Though London will be the first city to host the modern Games three times, the 2012 Olympics are being treated as London's chance to really shine. Both previous times the Olympic torch was lit in London, the city played the role of understudy, stepping in at the last minute. An eruption of Mount Vesuvius put the original 1908 host, Rome, out of commission, and, on short notice, London hosted a characteristically well-organized Olympics, even inaugurating the practice of constructing a new stadium for the Games. In 1948, London showcased British resolve and resilience, reinvigorating the Games after a 12-year hiatus during WWII.

THIRD TIME'S THE CHARM

London won the bid for the 30th Olympiad with a plan for the "greenest" games in history. The games have transformed the once-forgotten hinterlands of northeast London's Stratford neighborhood (not to be confused with Shakespeare's hometown, Stratford-Upon-Avon), from garbage dump to verdant Olympic showpiece. The Games' planners hope to make these Games entirely car-free, send no waste to landfills during the games, and plant more than 4000 trees to fill the Olympic Park and Village.

ICONIC OR MORONIC?

If you've seen the 2012 Olympics logo or mascots, you know that British wits will have many chances to flex their muscles by the time these Games are up. Since it was unveiled in June 2007, the London Olympics logo, a garishly colored, zig-zaggy rendering of the year 2012, has been the subject of controversy. Some think the logo looks uncomfortably like a broken swastika. Iran thinks it spells "Zion" and has threatened to boycott the Games in protest. For many people, though, it looks most like Lisa Simpson performing a certain sex act.

Almost as entertaining as the logo are the mascots. Whereas past Olympic planners drew upon their cities' cultural and biological heritage to design adorable mascots, London organizers were inspired by drops of molten steel from the factory in Bolton where the Olympic Stadium's girders were produced. Maybe that explains why "Wenlock" and "Mandeville" look so ridiculous.

Get Your Game On

The heart of the Olympics will be in the East London district of Stratford. The Olympic Park there contains the 80,000-seat **Olympic Stadium,** the sleek new **Aquatics Centre,** featuring a wavelike roof designed by Iraqi-British architect Zaha Hadid, and the 17,320-bed **Olympic Village.** The recently expanded Stratford Regional station connects the Park to central London by DLR, Underground, and bus.

There will also be plenty going on in the city center and hinterlands of London. Here's a quick guide to some of the other venues.

Arts and Culture

HORSE GUARDS PARADE

Sand is being trucked in to create a **beach volleyball** court on this parade ground between St. James's Park and a stretch of buildings that includes #10 Downing Street and the Horse Guards. Sadly, the arrangement is only temporary, and neither the Queen nor David Cameron responded to our request for a pick-up game.

HYDE PARK

Triathletes and marathon swimmers will dip into the waters of this famous park's Serpentine Lake. This will certainly be much more pleasant than going for a dip in the Thames.

EARLS COURT

There's no sand in this 1935 conference center in South Kensington and Chelsea, but it will make do with regular volleyball.

EXCEL

You'll be able to catch boxing, fencing, judo, wrestling, and (everyone's favorite) table tennis at this exhibition center in the London Docklands. From the Olympic Park or central London, take the DLR to get here.

GREENWICH PARK

A popular tourist destination even outside of Olympics season thanks to its glorious Old Royal Naval College (among other things), Greenwich Park will be going neigh-val rather than naval when equestrian events get going here. The venue is near Greenwich rail and DLR stations.

O_2 ARENA

This North Greenwich arena was originally built for the city's Millennium celebrations, and is now being repurposed as the venue for artistic gymnastics, trampoline, and wheelchair basketball. The venue is best reached by Tube, and there will be a shuttle running from Charlton. Note that, during the Games, it will be called the North Greenwich Arena thanks to the International Olympic Committee's hatred of all sponsors except their own.

WIMBLEDON

This one shouldn't be a surprise: the home of the All England Lawn Tennis and Croquet Club will open its pristine grass courts up to Olympic tennis competition. You can reach it by Tube, rail, or Tramlink (between Croydon and Wimbledon).

WEMBLEY STADIUM

Soccer players will duke it out at Wembley, six miles northwest of the city center. Coming from the north, the stadium can be reached by rail and London Overground; otherwise, you're best taking the Tube.

Spectating

You can find the most up-to-date information about purchasing tickets at www.tickets.london2012.com. If you haven't obtained tickets yet, expect slim pickings, but don't despair. You probably won't be able to get (or afford) tickets to the premier events, but you might be able to find some for the less popular ones. The cheapest £20 tickets are mainly for preliminary rounds of events, so you may be paying more for atmosphere than a good look at the competition. All tickets include a Travel Pass good for all London public transportation on the day of competition. Tickets cannot be sold legally without London 2012's permission, so make sure you deal with an official retailer.

Fortunately, there are plenty of opportunities to soak up the spirit of the games without having to buy a ticket. You can catch the cycling portion of the triathlon from Hyde Park. The marathon winds past many of London's famous monuments, including St. Paul's Cathedral and Big Ben—just make sure to claim your spot along the course early enough to get a good view. Our pick for the most absurd Olympic event, walking, as well as the cycling road races can also be viewed courseside without a ticket. Plans for the Olympic Park include "Henman Hills" from which visitors will be better able to view large screens broadcasting the games. Then of course, you can always drop into a pub and watch on the telly with some locals—probably the most authentically British way to experience the Games.

An Opening Ceremony to Remember

With Danny Boyle (director of *Slumdog Millionaire, Trainspotting,* and *28 Days Later*) as Artistic Director and Stephen Daldry (director of *Billy Elliot, The Hours,* and *The Reader*) on board as Executive Creative Producer, the 2012 Opening Ceremony arrives with a fine pedigree. Add to that a few ex-Spice Girls and you've got quite the heady (though perhaps incoherent) mix of talent. Here are our humble suggestions for Messers Boyle and Daldry as they set about designing a ceremony that will highlight all that's great in British culture.

- Team up the Spice Girls with Justin Bieber. Yes, he's not exactly British, but get ready to send tween girls into Nirvana.

- royal forever. Can you get the royal family involved? We'd love to see the Queen try her hand at archery. Even better, a beach volleyball match-up between William and Kate and Harry and... anyone but Camilla.

- Anything Harry Potter is golden. Bringing Dumbledore back to life gets you extra points.

- End it all with the giant *Monty Python* foot smashing everything.

THEATER

Ah, "theatre" (thee-ya-tah) in London. The city is renowned for its affordable performances—tickets for big musicals on the **West End** can be had for as little as £25, a pittance compared to the $100 tickets sold on Broadway. In the West End, London's main theater district, you'll find big musicals that stay in residence at a single theater for decades. Other theaters put on more cutting-edge works. Many pubs have live performance spaces where theater groups rehearse and perform for audiences that, after a few pints, tend to find the second act more confusing than the first. Some churches, like St. Paul's in Covent Garden, host shows during the summer. Only buy discounted tickets from booths with a circle and check mark symbol that says **STAR** on it; this stands for the Society of Tickets Agents and Retailers, and it vouches for the legitimacy of a discount booth.

🖼 Royal Court Theatre   SOUTH KENSINGTON AND CHELSEA
Sloane Sq.
☎020 7565 5000; www.royalcourttheatre.com

Famous for pushing the theatrical envelope, the Royal Court is the antidote to all the orchestral swoons and faux-opera sweeping through the West End. The Royal Court's 1956 production of John Osborne's *Look Back in Anger* (not to be confused with the Oasis song) is credited with single-handedly launching modern British drama. Royal is known as a writers' theater, purveying high-minded works for audiences that will appreciate them.

▶ ✴ ⊖Sloane Sq. Ⓢ Tickets M £10, Tu-Sa £12-28. Student discounts available on day of performance. ⏰ Box office open M-F 10am-6pm or until the doors open, Sa 10am-curtain (if there's a performance).

🖼 National Theatre   THE SOUTH BANK
Belvedere Rd.
☎020 7452 3400; www.nationaltheatre.org.uk

Opened in 1976 by appointment of the Queen, the National Theatre's multiple stages host new and classic British drama, including many premieres, revived lost classics from around the world, and a standard repertoire of Chekhov and Ibsen. Half the seats are sold for £10 at special Travelex discount shows.

▶ ✴ ⊖Waterloo. Turn right onto York Rd. and left onto Waterloo Rd. Ⓢ Tickets £10-44. ⏰ Box office open M-Sa 9:30am-8pm, Su noon-6pm.

🖼 The Old Vic   SOUTH LONDON
The Cut
☎0844 871 7628; www.oldvictheatre.com

This famous, stately theater was built in 1818 and has hosted the likes of Ralph Richardson and Laurence Olivier. Though showcasing a huge range of styles, the Old Vic focuses on the classics, including star-studded Shakespeare productions. Kevin Spacey has served as artistic director since 2003.

▶ ✴ ⊖Southwark. Turn right onto The Cut. Ⓢ Tickets £10-52. 100 tickets for each performance available to those under 25 for £12; call ahead to book. ⏰ Box office open M-Sa 10am-7pm on show days, 10am-6pm on non-show days.

The Young Vic   SOUTH LONDON
· 66 The Cut

☎020 7922 2922; www.youngvic.org

Formerly the studio space for the Old Vic, the Young Vic now puts on a variety of shows, generally edgier and more exciting than its more decorous parent theater down the road. Between its main stage and two studio spaces, the Young Vic also provides greater flexibility in stagings.

▶ ‡ ⊖Southwark. Turn right onto The Cut. Ⓢ Tickets £10-30. ⏰ Box office open M-Sa 10am-6pm.

Shakespeare's Globe   THE SOUTH BANK
21 New Globe Walk

☎020 7401 9919; www.shakespearesglobe.org

The original Globe burned down during a performance of *Henry VIII* in 1613, but this accurate reconstruction was opened near the original site in 1997. Much like the original theater, it has an open roof and standing area for "groundlings." Steeped in historical and artistic tradition, the Globe stages works by the Bard, along with two new plays per year. Their season only runs from April to October, but you probably wouldn't want to stand for three hours in the British winter, no matter how good the play.

▶ ‡ ⊖Southwark. Turn left onto Blackfriars Rd., right onto Southwark St., left onto Great Guildford St., right onto Park St., then left onto New Globe Walk. Ⓢ Standing £5; seats £15-35, under 18 £12-32. ⏰ Box office open M-Sa 10am-8pm, Su 10am-7pm.

POP AND ROCK

Clubs are expensive, and many pubs close at 11pm. Especially during the current recession, fewer young people are willing to shell out £10-15 to get into a club, especially since beers inside cost a further £4-5. To find the heart of London's nightlife, you have to get beyond the pub-and club surface and head into the darkened basements of bars and seismically loud music clubs. With a history of homegrown musical talent—including **The Rolling Stones, Radiohead,** and **The Clash,** all of the bands from the infamous **"British Invasion,"** and many of the best '90s pop groups—London's fantastic music scene goes way back. Today, it has all of the big name acts you'd expect a major city to draw, in addition to an underground focus on indie rock and a surprisingly ample dose of folk and blues.

👍 Koko

NORTH LONDON

1A Camden High St.

☎0870 432 5527; www.koko.uk.com

Koko's isn't a typical rock and roll venue. Originally a theater, then a cinema, then one of the BBC's first broadcasting locations, and then the famous Camden Palace Nightclub, Koko holds its 110-year history within its music-soaked red walls and gilded balconies. Bringing in mostly big-name indie acts, along with some pop and rock acts (they've had everyone from Madonna to Usher to Justice), Koko is one of the premier venues in London. It also hosts an indie night, with DJs and dancing, on Friday.

▶ 🚏 ⊖Mornington Crescent. Turn right onto Hampstead Rd. Koko is on the right. ℹ Tickets sold online. $ Concerts £10-30. Beer £3.50-4. For indie night, the 1st 100 people get in free. Cover £7; students £5 before midnight, £7 after. Cash only for in-person purchases. ⏰ Box office open noon-5pm on gig days. Indie night F 9:30pm-4am.

👍 Borderline

THE WEST END

Orange Yard, off Manette St.

☎020 7734 5547; venues.meanfiddler.com/borderline/home

This simple venue (which is also a fantastic club, see **Nightlife**) lacks the outlandish Art Deco trappings of other London concert halls, but it oozes the spirit of rock and roll from every beer-soaked wall and ear-blowing speaker. Big-name artists often play The Borderline when starting solo careers. Townes Van Zandt played his last show here; Eddie Vedder, Jeff Buckley, and Rilo Kiley have played here; and **👍Spinal Tap** performed here right after the movie came out. The amps go up to 11, the music's piping hot, and the location is prime.

▶ 🚏 ⊖Tottenham Court Rd. Turn right onto Charing Cross Rd., and right onto Manette St. $ Tickets £6-20. Pints £3.40. ⏰ Doors open daily 7pm. Tickets available at the Jazz Cafe box office M-Sa 10:30am-5:30pm.

HMV Apollo

WEST LONDON

15 Queen Caroline St.

☎020 8563 3800; www.hmvapollo.com

Like many of the big, architecturally stunning venues in London, the Art Deco HMV Apollo used to be a cinema. It was originally called the Hammersmith Odeon, and was the site of Bruce Springsteen's 1975 concert film. It's also hosted big acts like Oasis, R.E.M., Elton John, the Rolling Stones, and even the Beatles.

► ♿ ⊖Hammersmith. Apollo is opposite the Broadway Shopping Centre.
There are plenty of signs leading to it. *i* Call ☎08448 44 47 48 for tickets.
Ⓢ Ticket prices vary; check online for more info. 🕐 Box office open on
performance days 4pm-start of the show.

CLASSICAL MUSIC

If your tastes run more toward Mozart than the Arctic Monkeys,
there's still plenty of music in London for you. For free chamber
and classical music, check out London's churches—in particular,
St Martin-in-the-Fields—where students from famous music
schools often give professional-quality recitals for no charge.

⚓ Royal Opera House   THE WEST END
Bow St.
☎020 7304 4000; www.roh.org.uk

The glorious glass facade of the Royal Opera House makes it
look more like a train station than a theater, but that doesn't
mean that the opera performed here is anything less than world-
class. Tickets go on sale about two months before performances,
and it's a good idea to book early. Or you can wait for standby
tickets, which are offered four hours before performances for
half price, and are only £12 for students. The ROH also spon-

Mousey Mystery

Here's a fun trivia question: what's the longest-running stage
show in the world? Agatha Christie's *The Mousetrap.* Here's a
more relevant question: where is it playing? London!

After 58 years and over 23,000 performances, the show
has involved more than 380 actors, sold over 415 tons of ice
cream at intermission, and ironed more than 116 miles of shirts.
Don't waste your time at the discount ticket booths in Leicester
Sq.—though those are great for other shows, *The Mousetrap*
tickets are only on sale at St. Martin's Theatre box office. Because the show runs so often, it's hardly ever sold out, so you
can often show up 15min. before curtain and still get a seat. (St.
Martin's Theatre, West St. ☎0844 499 1515 ♿ Covent Garden
or Leicester Sq. Ⓢ Tickets £16-60. 🕐 Shows M 7:30pm, Tu 3
and 7:30pm, W-F 7:30pm, Sa 4 and 7:30pm. Box office open
M-Sa 10am-8pm.)

sors free outdoor film screenings. For information on dance performances at the ROH, see **Dance.**

▶ 🚌 ⊖Covent Garden. Turn right onto Long Acre, then right onto Bow St. $ Tickets £5-150. ⏰ Box office open M-Sa 10am-8pm.

Royal Albert Hall — SOUTH KENSINGTON AND CHELSEA

Kensington Gore

☎0845 401 5045; www.royalalberthall.com

Deep in the heart of South Kensington, the Royal Albert Hall, commissioned by Prince Albert, has been bringing the arts to London since 1871. The hall hosts some of the city's biggest concerts, including the **BBC Proms** classical festival (see **Festivals**) and a range of other phenomenal musical events. This is a historical and cultural experience that's not to be missed.

▶ 🚌 ⊖Knightsbridge. Turn left onto Knightsbridge and continue onto Kensington Rd., which becomes Kensington Gore. $ Tickets from £10. ⏰ Open daily 9am-9pm.

The London Coliseum — THE WEST END

33 St. Martin's Ln.

☎0871 472 0600; www.eno.org

Home to the **English National Opera,** the London Coliseum showcases new, cutting-edge ballet and opera. They also perform unique reworkings of classic opera productions, like a version of Donizetti's *L'Elisir d'Amore* set in a 1950s diner.

▶ 🚌 ⊖Charing Cross. Walk toward Trafalger Sq. on Duncannon St., turn right at the square onto St. Martin's Pl., and St. Martin's Ln. splits off to the right. *i* Sometimes students and other concessions can get discounted tickets 3hr. before the performance. $ Tickets £15-90. ⏰ Box office open M-Sa 10am-8pm on performance days, 10am-6pm on non-performance days.

JAZZ

👍 Ronnie Scott's — THE WEST END

47 Frith St.

☎020 7439 0747; www.ronniescotts.co.uk

Ronnie Scott's has been defining "hip" in Soho for the last 51 years. It was the first British club to host American jazz artists—everyone from Chick Corea to Tom Waits (ok, not jazz, but who's complaining?) has played here. The venue is all flickering candlelight and dulcet reds and blues. Black-and-white photos of jazz giants line the walls, and a diverse crowd imbibes cocktail creations like Jazz Medicine (Jägermeister, sloe gin, Dubonnet, fresh blackberries, and angostura bitters). The venue's cool, but the jazz is hot. Stop by if the Soho scene gets overwhelming.

▶ 🚶 ⊖Tottenham Court Rd. Turn onto Oxford St. with your back to Tottenham Court Rd., then left onto Soho St., right onto the square, and right onto Frith St. $ Cover £10, more for big acts. Cocktails £8.50-9. ⏰ Open M-F 6pm-3am, Sa 6:30pm-3am, Su noon-4pm and 6:30pm-midnight. Box office open M-F 10am-6pm, Sa noon-5pm.

The 606 Club — WEST LONDON

90 Lots Rd.

☎020 7352 5953; www.606club.co.uk

On quiet Lots Rd., opposite a foreboding abandoned factory, the 606 Club has been quietly hosting the best of the UK music scene since 1969. Properly underground (it's in a basement), the club is candlelit and closely packed. The music may be jazz, Latin, soul, gospel, R and B, and rock, and while the artists may be relatively unknown, they're almost always worth hearing.

▶ 🚶 Buss #22 from Sloane Sq. to Edith Grove/World's End. Continue walking on Kings Rd., turn left onto Tadema Rd., walk to the end, and turn right onto Lots Rd. *i* Non-members have to eat in order to drink. Check website for special Su afternoon lunch and show. $ Cover M-Th £10; F-Sa £12; Su lunch £8, evening £10. ⏰ Open M 7-11:30pm, Tu-W 7pm-12:30am, Th 7-11:30pm, F-Sa 8pm-1:30am, Su 12:30-4pm and 7-11pm.

DANCE

As with everything else in London, the dance scene is diverse, innovative, and first-rate. Come for the famous ballets at older venues like the Royal Opera House or stop by a smaller company for some contemporary dance.

Sadler's Wells — NORTH LONDON

Rosebery Ave.

☎0844 412 4300; www.sadlerswells.com

Sadler's Wells is renowned for stunning dance shows, including traditional ballet, contemporary dance, and dazzling Cuban ensembles. With multiple performance spaces, they might even all be on at the same time.

▶ 🚶 ⊖Angel. Turn left onto Upper St., then right onto Rosebery Ave. *i* Some shows offer student discounts. $ Tickets £10-55. ⏰ Box office open M-Sa 9am-8:30pm.

Royal Opera House
THE WEST END

Bow St.

☎020 7304 4000; www.roh.org.uk

The Royal Opera House may be opera-oriented in name, but in repertoire, it's split between opera and ballet. See the listing in **Classical Music** for more information.

▶ 🚇 Covent Garden. Turn right onto Long Acre, then right onto Bow St. $ Tickets £5-150. ⏰ Booking office open M-Sa 10am-8pm.

COMEDY

The English are famous for their dry, sophisticated yet sometimes ridiculous ("We are the knights who say 'Ni!'") sense of humor. This humor thrives in the standup and sketch comedy clubs throughout the city. Check *Time Out* for listings, and be warned that the city virtually empties of comedians come August when it's festival time in Edinburgh.

👍 Comedy Store
THE WEST END

1A Oxendon St.

☎0844 871 7699; www.thecomedystore.co.uk

Hands-down the most famous comedy venue in London, the Comedy Store made a name for itself in the '80s as a home for up-and-coming comedians like Jennifer Saunders, Dawn French, and Mike Myers (who was one of the founding members). Nowadays, visiting comics perform Thursday through Saturday, and the resident sketch-comedy team takes the stage on Wednesdays and Sundays. Tuesdays have standup on recent topical events, while the last Monday of the month hosts would-be comedians who are either encouraged or heckled by the audience. Famous comedians like Eddie Izzard have been known to pop in from time to time for impromptu performances.

▶ 🚇 Piccadilly Circus. Turn left onto Coventry, then right onto Oxendon. $ Tickets £14-20. ⏰ Box office open M-Th 6:30-9:30pm, F-Sa 6:30pm-1:15am, Su 6:30-9:30pm. Doors open daily 6:30pm. Shows usually 8 and 11pm.

Hen and Chickens Theatre
NORTH LONDON

109 St. Paul's Rd.

☎020 7704 2001; www.unrestrictedview.co.uk

You'll be treated to some of the most hilarious and quirky comedy around in this 50-seat venue, located above an Islington pub. Acts vary from standup to sketch-comedy groups. Past performers have included the Unexpected Items, a group that includes the originator of the sidesplitting "Gap Yah" video. Come in July to see comedians try out the material they're taking up to Edinburgh. Head down to the pub to enjoy a pint with the performers after the show.

▶ ✦ ⊖Highbury and Islington. Turn right and go down the road past the green. Ⓢ Tickets £6-8. ⏰ Performances usually at 7:30 or 9:30pm.

CINEMA

London is teeming with traditional cinemas, the most dominant of which are **Cineworld** (www.cineworld.co.uk) and **Odeon** (www.odeon.co.uk). But the best way to enjoy a film is in one of the hip repertory or luxury cinemas. *Time Out* publishes showtimes, as does www.viewlondon.co.uk.

▨ BFI Southbank   SOUTH BANK
Belvedere Rd.

☎020 7928 3232; www.bfi.org.uk

Hidden under Waterloo Bridge, the BFI Southbank is one of the most exciting repertory cinemas in London. Showcasing everything from current blockbusters to challenging foreign works, the BFI's slate of screenings keeps all cinema-lovers happy. It runs in themed "seasons" that focus on the work of a particular director, cinematographer, or actor. The Mediatheque is free and allows you to privately view films from their archives.

▶ ✦ ⊖Waterloo. Ⓢ £9.50, concessions £6.75. Tu £6.50. ⏰ Open daily 11am-11pm. Mediateque open Tu-F noon-8pm, Sa-Su 12:30pm-8pm.

Riverside Studios   WEST LONDON
Crisp Rd.

☎020 8237 1111; www.riversidestudios.co.uk

Frequently showing films in old-school double features, Riverside Studios specializes in foreign films, art-house flicks, and classics. The building is a hotbed for other culture as well, featuring an exhibition space, live theater performances, a popular cafe, and a bar.

▶ ✦ ⊖Hammersmith. Take the south exit and pass the Hammersmith Apollo. Continue to follow Queen Caroline St. and turn left onto Crisp Rd. 𝑖 Ethernet access in cafe. Ⓢ Tickets £8.50, concessions £7.50. ⏰ Open M-F 8:30am-11pm, Sa 10am-11pm, Su 10am-10:30pm. Box office open daily noon-9pm.

FESTIVALS

Come summer, it seems like every park in London hosts a festival each weekend. There are folk festivals, hard-rock festivals, indie/pop/hip-hop festivals, food festivals... you name it. It's impossible to keep track of them all, so keep an eye out for posters around the city.

⬛ BBC Proms   SOUTH KENSINGTON AND CHELSEA

Kensington Gore

☎0845 401 5045; www.bbc.co.uk/proms

The Proms are a world-famous classical music festival put on by the BBC in the Royal Albert Hall. If you're thinking teenagers in taffeta, think again. "Prom" stands for "Promenade Concert"—a performance at which much of the audience only has standing-room tickets. There's at least one performance every day at the Royal Albert Hall, plus around 70 other events and discussions throughout the city. All the performances are broadcast for free.

▶ ⚡ ⊖Knightsbridge. Turn left onto Knightsbridge, then continue onto Kensington Rd., which becomes Kensington Gore. ⓢ Tickets from £10. ⏰ July-Sept.

London Literary Festival   THE SOUTH BANK

Southbank Centre, Belvedere Rd.

☎0844 847 9939; www.londonlitfest.com

Some of the world's most famous poets, novelists, musicians,

Like Proper English Blokes

So you're looking for a reason to party, and you want to do it with a bit of English class? One of the best ways to really experience English life at its poshest is to attend the Henley Royal Regatta, which takes place in Henley-on-Thames (40 mi. west of London) during the first weekend of July. In the wonderful world of rowing, this race is about as important as it gets, and it was even featured in *The Social Network.* But if you're like the rest of us, you can simply use it as an excuse to dress prep-chic (think matching striped jackets and ties), pretend you're sophisticated enough to judge each rower's form, and sip Pimm's by the river.

Arts and Culture

and scientists (it's quite the interdisciplinary fest) assemble at the South Bank Centre every July for this literary extravaganza. The festival also hosts writing workshops; you can download podcasts of past events on their website.

► 🚏 ⊖Waterloo. Turn right onto York Rd. and then left onto Waterloo Rd. The festival is held on the embankment before York Bridge. $ Ticket prices free-£15, concessions often ½ off. ⏰ Call daily 9am-8pm. Book through Royal Festival Hall Ticket Office daily 10am-8pm.

Shopping

London is known as one of the shopping capitals of the world. Knightsbridge's famous department stores fight to keep the tradition of shopping class alive, Soho offers vintage clothing stores and independent record shops, and the East End is filled with fun boutiques. Notting Hill is famous for Portobello Market, but even on off-market days, the road has a host of cute secondhand shops. Chelsea is for those with a bit more money and a serious commitment to shopping. For you literary junkies, John Sandoe's is our favorite bookstore in the city. Shopping is a significant part of London tourism, but if you're broke and have no extra room in your backpack, you can always just browse the day away at Harrods.

Budget Shopping

We aren't going to lie to you—it's very easy to come to London and leave with a significantly lighter checkbook. If you're too poor to buy anything, you may feel dissatisfied with your financial ineptitude after window-shopping at Harrods. Don't let this happen to you. The budget traveler should desert the famed South Kensington and Chelsea shopping districts and instead head to the outskirts, where you will find surprisingly quality items for disturbingly low prices.

BOOKSTORES

📓 John Sandoe Books   SOUTH KENSINGTON AND CHELSEA

10 Blacklands Terr.

☎020 7589 9473; www.johnsandoe.com

The stairs to the second-floor fiction section at John Sandoe reminds visitors of the joy of independent bookstores. There's barely space for peoples' feet, as half of each stair is taken up by piles of carefully selected books. A cracked leather chair presides over bookcases so packed with masterworks and little-known gems that they're layered with moving shelves. The knowledge-able, personable staff is ever-ready to dole out excellent sugges-tions. Book-lovers beware: it's easy to spend a day (and a pile of cash) in this shop.

▶ ⚡ ⊖Sloane Sq. Exit the Tube and go straight down Sloane Sq. Veer left onto King's Rd., and turn right at Blacklands Terr. 🕐 Open M-Tu 9:30am-5:30pm, W 9:30am-7:30pm, Th-Sa 9:30am-5:30pm, Su noon-6pm.

📓 Skoob   MARLEBONE AND BLOOMSBURY

66 The Brunswick, off Marchmont St.

☎020 7278 8760; www.skoob.com

The Brunswick Center is all white and shiny and full of bougie stores—not the place where you'd expect to find a haven for dusty secondhand books. And yet here is Skoob, a basement shop where most books are £1-4. They come from pretty much any genre you can think of: travel writing (if *Let's Go* has in-spired you), fiction, mysteries, history, biographies, you name it. They have over a million more books in their warehouse, thousands of which can be ordered from their website. As if that wasn't enough, they offer a 10% student discount.

▶ ⚡ ⊖Russell Sq. Turn right and then left up Marchmont St. Skoob is at the far end of Brunswick, on the right. 🕐 Open M-Sa 10:30am-8pm, Su 10:30am-6pm.

ART

Marcus Campbell Art Books   THE SOUTH BANK

43 Holland St.

☎020 7261 0111; www.marcuscampbell.co.uk

Close enough in theme and proximity to the Tate Modern to

be considered its unofficial bookstore, Marcus Campbell Art Books sells a wide variety of exhibition catalogues (many for £1-2), and rare and expensive art books (up to £3000). A fun store for browsing and shopping alike, with books so beautiful they're works of art in themselves.

▶ ‡ ⊖Southwark. Turn left onto Blackfriars Rd., then right onto Southwark St. Next turn left onto Sumner, and left onto Holland St. 🕐 Open M-Sa 10:30am-6:30pm, Su noon-6pm.

Southbank Printmakers   THE SOUTH BANK
Unit 12 Gabriels Wharf, 56 Upper Ground
☎020 7928 8184; www.southbank-printmakers.com

Every 5min., someone in London is sold a cheap work of bad, tourist-trap art. Southbank Printmakers aim to stop this grave injustice. The artist cooperative has been around for 10 years, producing quality lino cuts, wood cuts, etchings, and monoprints at a range of prices. Many of the prints are London-themed, making for original and affordable souvenirs.

▶ ‡ ⊖Southwark. Turn left onto Blackfriars Rd., left onto Stamford St., and right onto Duchy St. 🕐 Open in summer M-F 11:30am-6:30pm, Sa-Su 10am-8pm; in winter M-F 11:30am-5:30pm, Sa-Su 10am-7pm.

MUSIC

🖼 Music and Video Exchange   HYDE PARK TO NOTTING HILL
42 Notting Hill Gate
☎020 7221 2793; www.mgeshops.com

Music and Video Exchange will provide hours (if not days) of entertainment to any audiophile. The staff engage in constant *High Fidelity*-esque conversations and practically ooze musical knowledge, while customers browse through vinyl, CDs, and cassettes in the bargain area. Upstairs in the rarities section, you can find anything from a £12 original vinyl of the Rolling Stones' *Get Yer Ya-Ya's Out!* to the original German sleeve for the Beatles' *Let it Be*. Customers can trade in their own stuff in exchange for cash or—in a move betraying MVE's cold-hearted understanding of a music-lover's brain—twice the cash amount in store vouchers.

▶ ‡ ⊖Notting Hill Gate. Walk out the south entrance of the Tube and go down Notting Hill Gate. 🕐 Open daily 10am-8pm.

Shopping

▧ Sister Ray

THE WEST END

34-35 Berwick St.

☎020 7734 3297; www.sisterray.co.uk

An old-school record shop of the best kind, Sister Ray's stellar staff is adept at creating musical matches-made-in-heaven. Hip, cheap books about music line the check-out counter, and listening stations are located throughout the store. The store also buys, so if you want to sell your classic punk records to fund the next leg of your vacation, this is the place for you.

▶ ⌗ ⊖Tottenham Court Rd. Turn left onto Oxford St., left onto Wardour St., and left onto Berwick St. ⏰ Open M-Sa 10am-8pm, Su noon-6pm.

(E.T.) Phone Home

In the highly unlikely case that London's internet connection, cell-phone reception, and mail-carrying owls are all out of commission when you need them, you can always step into one of Britain's iconic red telephone boxes. Though these booths were first deployed in London in 1926 for obvious purposes, they have now become more of a novelty for tourists and are utilized for all kinds of non-telephone purposes. Some of the more interesting ones include:

- **BOOK/MOVIE PROPS.** In the **Harry Potter** series, a red telephone box provides a way into the Ministry of Magic. However, given the strange smell wafting about in many of London's actual telephone booths, floo powder might be a better way to travel.

- **ARTWORK.** In **Kingston upon Thames,** several disused red telephone boxes are lined up, all tipped sideways, in an arrangement resembling falling dominoes. This artwork, called *Out of Order,* was commissioned in 1988, when this sort of wackiness was all the rage.

- **COMMERCIAL PRODUCTS.** Want your very own red telephone booth? You can now order a replica online for prices ranging from your arm and leg to your first-born child.

- **MINI-LIBRARY.** You know Britain has too many cell phones—or too few libraries—when they start to convert telephone kiosks into libraries. Located in **Westbury-sub-Mendip,** this mini literary haven is fairly busy. It's also 150 miles west of London, so probably not worth the daytrip.

Shopping

The Schott Music Shop THE WEST END
48 Great Marlborough St.
☎020 7292 6090; www.schottmusic.co.uk

Opened in 1857, Schlott is the oldest sheet-music shop in London. This quiet, spacious store sells everything from the Beatles to Bartók. Especially notable to music-starved travelers are the three practice rooms beneath the shop (each with a baby grand Steinway) available to rent by the hour.

▶ ♯ ⊖Oxford Circus. Turn left onto Regent St., and left onto Great Marlborough St. *i* 10% student discount on print music. Ⓢ Practice rooms £10 per hr. before noon, £12 per hr. noon-6pm, £15 per hr. after 6pm. ⏰ Open M-F 10am-6:30pm, Sa 10am-6pm.

MARKETS

▨ Borough Market THE SOUTH BANK
Southwark St.
www.boroughmarket.org.uk

Anyone who bemoans the food scene in London has never been to Borough Market. In a tangle of stalls and shops under a set of railway viaducts, traders sell the best in fresh produce, meat, and artisanal products. Looking for rare Italian sausage, the juiciest English strawberries, or decadent French cheese? Find them here. Or just take a wander and discover things you never knew you needed, like truffled *mortadella* and tiny brioches. The people who work here are incredibly knowledgeable and ready to recommend an item or a recipe. And in addition to the food stands, there are a number of restaurants and cafes that share in the gourmet aura of the market.

▶ ♯ ⊖London Bridge. Exit the Tube and walk down Southwark St. away from the river. The market will be on your right, starting where Southwark St. and Borough High St. split off. ⏰ Open Th 11am-5pm, F noon-6pm, Sa 8am-5pm.

Old Spitalfields Market EAST LONDON
Commercial St.
www.oldspitalfieldsmarket.com

This is the sort of market that clearly belongs in the East End, selling stylish vintage clothes, quirky antiques, and an array of art. It's a mix of stores and stalls offering everything from a quick manicure to a spicy kebab. They're not all open every day, but Sundays are the busiest and have the best variety of vendors. If you're looking for antiques, Thursday is your day.

Shopping

▶ ✇ ⊖Shoreditch High St. Make a left down Commercial St. 🕧 Opening times vary per vendor, but most are open daily 10am-5pm.

DEPARTMENT STORES

🏪 Harrods   SOUTH KENSINGSTON AND CHELSEA

87-135 Brompton Rd.

☎020 7730 1234; www.harrods.com

An ode to the experience of shopping, Harrods is probably the most famous department store on the planet. Packed with faux-hieroglyphs, a "Room of Luxury" (and its sequel, "Room of Luxury II"), and just about anything you could ever want to buy, Harrods is as much a sight to see as it is a place to shop. The prices and the people who pay, may be the most entertaining part of it all. Be sure to check out the toy section—you'll struggle to contain your inner child. Don't miss the food court's candy section, where they sell chocolate shoes (£84 for a pair). On the bottom floor, they sell "Personalised Classics," which enable you to substitute names for the ones already in a given book. Who needs "Romeo and Juliet" when you could have "Fred and Agnes?" "Fred, Fred, wherefore art thou Fred?" The answer: in shopping heaven.

▶ ✇ ⊖Knightsbride. Take the Harrods Exit. 🕧 Open M-Sa 10am-8pm, Su 11:30am-6pm.

Liberty   THE WEST END

Great Marlborough St.

☎020 7734 1234; www.liberty.co.uk

No, this epic Tudor building isn't a giant pub or a replica of a Shakespearean theater; it's a department store that, since the 19th century, has been presenting the best in art and design to its customers. Back in the day, this meant working in the Art Nouveau and Arts and Crafts styles—they were so successful that in Italy, they're just referred to as *Stile Liberty*. Today, you can buy everything from clothes to plates bearing the store's iconic prints. There are also men's and women's collections from fashion-forward designers like Alexander Wang and Vivienne Westwood. Don't miss the array of ribbons, feathers, and tulle in the haberdashery section.

▶ ✇ ⊖Oxford Circus. Go down Regent St. and turn left onto Great Marlborough St. 🕧 Open M-Sa 10am-9pm, Su noon-6pm.

Shopping

Essentials

You don't have to be a rocket scientist to plan a good trip. (It might help, but it's not required.) You do, however, need to be well prepared, and that's what we can do for you. Essentials is the chapter that gives you all the nitty-gritty you need to know for your trip: the hard information gleaned from 50 years of collective wisdom and several months of furious fact-checking. Planning your trip? Check. Where to find Wi-Fi? Check. The dirt on public transportation? Check. We've also thrown in communications info, safety tips, and a climate chart, just for good measure. Plus, for overall trip-planning advice from what to pack (money and as little underwear as possible) to how to take a good passport photo (it's physically impossible; consider airbrushing), you can also check out the Essentials section of www.letsgo.com.

So, flick through this chapter before you leave so you know what documents to bring, while you're on the plane so you know how you'll be getting from the airport to your accommodation, and when you're on the ground so you can find a laundromat to solve all your 3am stain-removal needs. This chapter may not always be the most scintillating read, but it just might save your life.

RED TAPE

Documents and Formalities

We're going to fill you in on visas and work permits, but don't forget the most important one of all: your passport. **Don't forget your passport!**

Visas

Those lucky enough to be EU citizens do not need a visa to globetrot through Britain. You citizens of Australia, Canada, New Zealand, and the US do not need a visa for stays of up to six months. Those staying longer than six months may apply for a longer-term visa; consult an embassy or consulate for more information. The rules for citizens of other non-EU countries vary. Check www.ukvisas.gov.uk to find out what you need to do.

Work Permits

Admittance to a country as a traveler does not include the right to work, which is authorized only by a work permit. For more information, see the **Beyond Tourism** chapter.

Embassies and Consulates

- **BRITISH CONSULAR SERVICES IN AUSTRALIA: Consulate General.** (Level 16, Gateway Bldg., Macquarie Pl., Sydney, NSW 2000 ☎02 9247 7521; www.ukinaustralia.fco.gov.uk ☒ Open M-F 9am-12:30pm and 1:30-5pm.)

- **BRITISH CONSULAR SERVICES IN CANADA: Consulate General.** (777 Bay St., Ste. 2800, College Park, Toronto, ON M5G 2G2 ☎416-593-1290; www.ukincanada.fco.gov.uk ☒ Open M-F 9am-4:30pm.)

- **BRITISH CONSULAR SERVICES IN IRELAND: Embassy.** (29 Merrion Rd., Ballsbridge, Dublin 4 ☎01 205 3700; www. britishembassyinireland.fco.gov.uk ☒ Open M-Th 9am-12:45pm and 2-4:15pm, F 9am-12:45pm and 2-5pm.)

- **BRITISH CONSULAR SERVICES IN NEW ZEALAND: High Commission.** (44 Hill St., Wellington, 6011 ☎04 924 2888; www. ukinnewzealand.fco.gov.uk ⏰ Open M-F 8:45am-5pm.)

- **BRITISH CONSULAR SERVICES IN THE US: Consulate General.** (845 Third Ave., New York, NY 10022 ☎212-745-0200; www.ukinusa.fco.gov.uk ⏰ Open M-Th 9am-noon, Th-F 9am-noon.) Other consulate generals in Atlanta, Boston, Chicago, Denver, Houston, Los Angeles, Miami, and San Francisco, and the embassy in Washington, DC.

- **AUSTRALIAN CONSULAR SERVICES IN LONDON: High Commission.** (Australia House, Strand ☎020 7379 4334; www. uk.embassy.gov.au ⏰ Open M-F 9am-5pm.)

- **CANADIAN CONSULAR SERVICES IN LONDON: High Commission.** (Macdonald House, 1 Grosvenor Sq. ☎020 7258 6600; www.canadainternational.gc.ca/united_kingdom-royaume_uni ⏰ Open M-F 9:30am-1pm.)

- **IRISH CONSULAR SERVICES IN LONDON: Embassy.** (17 Grosvenor Pl. ☎020 7589 8450; www.embassyofireland.co.uk ⏰ Open M-F 9:30am-5pm.)

- **NEW ZEALAND CONSULAR SERVICES IN LONDON: Embassy.** (New Zealand House, 80 Haymarket ☎020 7839 4580; www. nzembassy.com/united-kingdom ⏰ Open M-F 9am-5pm.)

- **AMERICAN CONSULAR SERVICES IN LONDON: Embassy.** (24 Grosvenor Sq. ☎020 7499 9000; http://london.usembassy. gov ⏰ Open M-F 8:30am-5:30pm.)

Did You Know...?

Though many have GPS systems in their cars, the 21,000 London black-cab drivers all had to pass a very intense test called "The Knowledge." In order to earn a license vaid for the entire city, would-be cabbies must prove they know the best routes for all of the 25,000 streets within a six-mile radius of Charing Cross Station. So, if you're ever lost, seek out a black cab and ask for directions.

Essentials

MONEY

Getting Money from Home

Stuff happens. When stuff happens, you might need some money. When you need some money, the easiest and cheapest solution is to have someone back home make a deposit to your bank account. Otherwise, consider one of the following options.

Wiring Money

Arranging a **bank money transfer** means asking a bank back home to wire money to a bank in London. This is the cheapest way to transfer cash, but it's also the slowest and most agonizing, usually taking several days or more. Note that some banks may only release your funds in local currency, potentially sticking you with a poor exchange rate; inquire about this in advance.

Money transfer services like **Western Union** are faster and more convenient than bank transfers—but also much pricier. Western Union has many locations worldwide. To find one, visit www. westernunion.com or call the appropriate number: in Australia ☎1800 173 833, in Canada 800-235-0000, in the UK 0808 234 9168, in the US 800-325-6000. Money transfer services are also available to **American Express** cardholders and at selected **Thomas Cook** offices. Remember to bring your ID to receive the money!

US State Department (US Citizens Only)

In serious emergencies only, the US State Department will help your family or friends forward money within hours to the nearest consular office, which will then disburse it according to instructions for a US$30 fee. If you wish to use this service, you must contact the Overseas Citizens Services division of the US State Department. (☎+1-202-501-4444, from US 888-407-4747)

Withdrawing Money

To use a debit or credit card to withdraw money from a cash machine (ATM) in Europe, you must have a four-digit Personal Identification Number (PIN). If your PIN is longer than four digits, ask your bank whether you can just use the first four or whether you'll need a new one. Credit cards don't usually come with PINs, so if you intend to hit up ATMs in Europe with a credit card to get cash advances, call your credit card company before leaving to request one.

One of the most expensive cities on the planet, London is chock-full of ATMs. Don't worry—there will most likely be an ATM near to you if you plan on staying within the city limits. A capitalist's heaven, London is also home to some of the biggest bosses in the banking business such as Barclay's, Natwest, Lloyd's, and the Royal Bank of Scotland. For tourist purposes, these are all essentially the same, unless your home bank has a special relationship with one of them.

Tipping and Bargaining

Tips in restaurants are sometimes included in the bill (sometimes as a "service charge"). If gratuity is not included, you should tip your server about 10%. Taxi drivers should receive a 10% tip, and bellhops and chambermaids usually expect £1-3. To the great relief of many budget travelers, tipping is not expected at pubs and bars in Britain (unless you are trying to get jiggy with the bartender). Bargaining is practically unheard of in the upscale shops that overrun London. Don't try it (unless you happen to be at a street market, or feel particularly belligerent).

Taxes

The UK has a 20% **value added tax (VAT),** a sales tax applied to everything but food, books, medicine, and children's clothing. The tax is included in the amount indicated on the price tag. The prices stated in *Let's Go* include VAT. Upon exiting Britain, non-EU citizens can reclaim VAT (minus an administrative fee) through the Retail Export Scheme, although the process is time-consuming, annoying, and may not be worth it, except for large purchases. You can obtain refunds only for goods you take out of the country (not for accommodations or noms). Participating shops display a "Tax-Free Shopping" sign and may have a minimum purchase of £50-100 before they offer refunds. To claim a refund, fill out the form you are given in the shop and present it with the goods and receipts at customs upon departure (look for the Tax-Free Refund desk at the airport). At peak times, this process can take up to an hour. You must leave the country within three months of your purchase in order to claim a refund, and you must apply before leaving the UK.

GETTING THERE

By Plane

London's main airport is **Heathrow** (LHR; ☎0844 335 1801; www.heathrowairport.com), commonly regarded as one of the world's busiest airports. The cheapest way to get from Heathrow to central London is on the Tube. The two Tube stations servicing Heathrow form a loop at the end of the **Piccadilly** line, which runs to central London. (⏰ 1hr.; every 5min. M-Sa 5am-11:54pm, Su 5:46am-10:37pm.) **Heathrow Express** (☎084 5600 1515; www.heathrowexpress.com) runs between Heathrow and Paddington station four times per hour. The trip is significantly shorter (though comparably pricier) than many of the alternatives, clocking in at around 15-20min. ($ £16.50 when purchased online, £18 from station, £23 on board. ⏰ 1st train departs daily around 5:10am.) The **Heathrow Connect** also runs to Paddington but is cheaper and takes longer, since it makes five stops on the way to and from the airport. There are two trains per hour, and the trip takes about 25min.

The **National Express** (☎08717 818 178; www.nationalexpress.com) bus runs between Victoria Coach Station and Heathrow three times per hour. Though cheap and often simpler than convoluted Underground trips, the buses are subject to the travails of London traffic. Posing a similar traffic threat, **taxis** from the airport to Victoria cost around £60 and take around 45min. In short, they aren't worth it.

Getting to **Gatwick Airport** (LGW; ☎0844 335 1802; www.gatwickairport.com) takes around 30min., making it less convenient than Heathrow but less hectic, too. The swift and affordable train services that connect Gatwick to the city make the trip a little easier. The **Gatwick Express** train runs non-stop service to Victoria station. You can buy tickets in terminals, at the station, or on the train itself. (☎0845 850 1530; www.gatwickexpress.com $ 1-way £15.20; 2-way £25.80. Round-trip ticket valid for a month. ⏰ 35min., every 15min. 5:50am-12:35am.)

National Express runs buses from the North and South terminals of Gatwick to London. The National Express bus (☎0871 781 8178; www.nationalexpress.com) takes approximately 1½hr., and buses depart for London Victoria hourly. Taxis take about 1hr. to reach central London. **easyBus** (☎084 4800 4411; www.easybus.co.uk) runs every 15min. from North and South terminals to Earls Court and West Brompton. (Ⓢ Tickets from £20. ⓪ 65min., every 15min.)

By Train

Europeans are far ahead of Americans in terms of train travel, and London offers several ways to easily reach other European destinations. Multiple train companies pass through the city. The biggest are **Eurostar** (☎08432 186 186; www.eurostar.com), which travels to Paris and Brussels, and **National Rail** (☎08457 48 49 50; www.nationalrail.co.uk), which oversees lines running throughout the United Kingdom. Train travel in Britain is generally reliable but can be unreasonably expensive. Booking tickets weeks in advance can lead to large savings, but spur-of-the-moment train trips to northern cities could cost more than £100.

By Bus

Bus travel is another, frequently cheaper, option. **Eurolines** (☎08717 818 181; www.eurolines.co.uk ⓪ Open 8am-8pm.) is Europe's largest coach network, servicing 500 destinations throughout Europe. Many buses leave from **Victoria Coach Station,** at the mouth of Elizabeth St. just off of Buckingham Palace Rd. Many coach companies, including **National Express, Eurolines,** and **Megabus,** operate from Victoria Coach. National Express is the only scheduled coach network in Britain and can be used for most intercity travel and for travel to and from various airports. It can also be used to reach Scotland and Wales.

GETTING AROUND

Though there are daily interruptions to Tube service, the controlling network, **Transport of London,** does a good job of keeping travelers aware of these disruptions to service. Each station will have posters listing interruptions to service, and you can check service online at www.tfl.gov.uk or the 24hr. travel information service (☎0843 222 1234). The website also has a journey planner that can plot your route using any public transport service ("TFL" is a verb here). Memorize that website. Love that website. Though many people in the city stay out into the wee hours, the Tube doesn't have the same sort of stamina. When it closes around midnight, night owls have two choices: cabs or **night buses.**

Travel Passes

Travel passes are almost guaranteed to save you money. The passes are priced based on the number of zones they serve (the more zones, the more expensive), but zone 1 encompasses central London and you'll rarely need to get past zone 2. If someone offers you a secondhand ticket, don't take it. There's no real way to verify whether it's valid—plus, it's illegal. Under 16s get free travel on buses. Passengers ages 11-15 enjoy reduced fares on the Tube with an Oyster photocard. Students 18 and older must study full time (at least 15hr. per week over 14 weeks) in London to qualify for the Student Photocard, which enables users to save 30% on adult travel cards and bus passes. It's worth it if you're staying for an extended period of time (study-abroad kids, we're looking at you).

Oyster cards enable you to pay in a variety of ways. Fares come in peak (M-F 6:30-9:30am and 4-7pm) and off-peak varieties and are, again, distinguished by zone. Oysters let you "pay as you go," meaning that you can store credit on an as-needed basis. Using an Oyster card will save you up to 50% off a single ticket. Remember to tap your card both on entering and leaving the station. You can use your card to add Travelcards, which allow unlimited travel on one day. This will only be cost-effective if you plan to use the Tube a lot. They cost £8.20 for anytime travel or £6.60 for off-peak travel. You can top up your Oyster at one of the infinite off-licences, marked by the Oyster logo, that scatter the city.

Season Tickets are weekly, monthly, and annual Travelcards that work on all public transport, and can be purchased inside Tube stations. They yield unlimited (within zone) use for their duration. (Ⓢ Weekly rates for zones 1-2 £27.50, monthly £106.)

By Underground

Most stations have Tube maps on the walls and free pocket maps. The Tube map barely reflects an above-ground scale, though, and should not be used for even the roughest estimation of walking directions (seriously). Platforms are organized by line, and will have the colors of the lines serviced and their names on the wall. The colors of the poles inside the trains correspond with the line, and trains will often have their end destination displayed on the front. This is an essential service when your line splits. Many platforms will have a digital panel indicating ETAs for the trains and sometimes type and final destination. When transferring within a station, just follow the clearly marked routes.

The Tube runs from Monday to Saturday from approximately 5:30am (though it depends on station and line) until around midnight. If you're taking a train within 30min. of these times (before or after), you'll want to check the signs in the ticket hall for times of the first and last train. The Tube runs less frequently on Sunday, with many lines starting service after 6am. Around 6pm on weekdays, many of the trains running out of central London are packed with the after-work crowd. It's best to avoid these lines at this time of day.

You can buy tickets from ticket counters (though these often have lines at bigger stations) or at machines in the stations. You need to swipe your ticket at the beginning of the journey and then again to exit the Tube. Random on-train checks will ask you to present a valid ticket to avoid the £50 penalty fee (reduced to £25 if you pay in under 21 days).

The **Overground** is a new addition to the London public transportation scene. It services parts of the city past zone 1 where Tube lines are sparse, and is particularly useful in East London. Fares and rules are the same as the Tube; you can just think of it as another line, except with a better view.

By Bus

While slower than the Tube for long journeys (thanks to traffic and more frequent stops), buses are useful for traveling short distances covered by a few stops (and several transfers) on the Tube.

Bus stops frequently post lists of buses servicing the stop as well as route maps and maps of the area indicating nearby stops. These maps are also very helpful for finding your way around a neighborhood. Buses display route numbers.

Every route and stop is different, but buses generally run every 5-15min. beginning around 5:30am and ending around midnight. After day bus routes have closed, **night buses** take over. These typically operate similar routes to their daytime equivalents, and their numbers are usually prefixed with an N (N13, for instance). Some buses run 24hr. services. If you're staying out past the Tube's closing time, you should plan your night-bus route or bring cab fare. (Ⓢ Single rides £2.20.)

PRACTICALITIES

For all the hostels, cafes, museums, and bars we list, we know some of the most important places you visit during your trip might actually be more mundane. Whether it's a tourist office, free Wi-Fi hot spot, or post office, these practicalities are vital to a successful trip, and you'll find all you need right here.

- **TOURIST OFFICES:** The main central tourist office in London is the **Britain and London Visitor Centre (BLVC).** (1 Regent St.; www.visitbritain.com 🪧 ⊖Piccadilly Circus. ⏰ Open Apr-Sept M 9:30am-6pm, Tu-F 9am-6:30pm, Sa-Su 10am-4pm; Oct-Mar M 9:30am-6:30pm, Tu-F 9am6pm, Sa-Su 10am-4pm.) Also useful is the **London Information Centre.** (Leicester Sq. ☎020 7292 2333; www.londoninformationcentre.com 🪧 ⊖Leicester Sq. ⏰ Open daily 8am-midnight.)

- **TOURS: Original London Walks** offers walking tours with themes like "Jack the Ripper" and "Harry Potter." (☎020 7624 9255; www.walks.com $ £8, students and over 65 £6.)

- **CURRENCY EXCHANGE: Thomas Cook.** (30 St James's St. ☎084 5308 9570 ⏰ Open M-Tu 10am-5:30pm, Th-F 10am-5:50pm.)

- **CREDIT CARD SERVICES: American Express** (www.amex-travelresources.com) has locations at 78 Brompton Rd. (☎084 4406 0046 🪧 ⊖Knightsbridge. ⏰ Open M-Tu 9am-5:30pm, W 9:30am-5:30pm, Th-F 9am-5:30pm, Sa 9am-4pm.) and 30-31 Haymarket. (☎084 4406 0044 🪧 ⊖Piccadilly Circus. ⏰ Open M-F 9am-5:30pm.)

- **GLBT RESOURCES:** The official **LGBT Tourist office** offers information on everything from saunas to theater discounts. (25 Frith St.; www.gaytouristoffice.co.uk 🪧 ⊖Leicester Sq.) **Boyz** (www.boyz.co.uk) lists gay events in London as well as an online version of its magazine. **Gingerbeer** (www.gingerbeer.co.uk) is a guide for lesbian and bisexual women with events listings. **Time Out London's** magazine and website (www.timeout.com/london) also provide a good overview of the city's GLBT establishments and the city in general.

- **TICKET OFFICES: Albermarle of London** agency provides

official tickets for all major West End theatre productions.
Book tickets via web, phone, or visiting the office. (5th fl.,
Medius House, 63-69 New Oxford St. ☎020 7379 1357;
www.albemarle-london.com ✪ Open M-F 8am-8:30pm, Sa
8:30am-8pm, Su 10am-6pm.)

- **INTERNET:** Wi-Fi abounds in this technologically advanced
  city. Most cafes provide internet access. Chains like **Starbucks**
  (www.starbucks.co.uk) and **McDonald's** (www.mcdonalds.
  co.uk) almost always have free Wi-Fi. Other chains with
  Wi-Fi include **The Coffee Republic** (www.coffeerepublic.
  co.uk), **Wetherspoon** (www.jdwetherspoon.co.uk), and **Pret
  a Manger** (www.pret.com). Public areas also have Wi-Fi. The
  area between **Upper Street and Holloway Road,** also known as
  The Technology Mile, is the longest stretch of free internet in
  the city.

- **POST OFFICES: Trafalgar Square Post Office.** (24-28 William
  IV St. ☎020 7484 9305 ⚐ ⊖Charing Cross. ✪ Open M
  8:30am-6:30pm, Tu 9:15am-6:30pm, W-F 8:30am-6:30pm,
  Sa 9am-5:30pm.)

SAFETY AND HEALTH

General Advice

In any type of crisis, the most important thing to do is **stay calm.**
Your country's embassy abroad is usually your best resource in
an emergency; registering with that embassy upon arrival in the
country is a good idea. The government offices listed in the **Travel
Advisories** feature at the end of this section can provide information on the services they offer their citizens in case of emergencies
abroad.

Police

Police are a common presence in London, and there are many
police stations scattered throughout the city. There are two types
of police officers in Britain: regular officers with full police pow-
ers, and police community support officers (PCSO), who have
limited police power and focus on community maintenance and
safety. The national emergency number is ☎999.

Essentials

Drugs and Alcohol

The Brits love to drink, so the presence of alcohol is unavoidable. In trying to keep up with the locals, remember that the Imperial pint is 20 oz., as opposed to the 16oz. US pint. The legal age at which you can buy alcohol in the UK is 18 (16 for buying beer and wine with food at a restaurant).

Despite what you may have seen on *Skins,* use and possession of hard drugs is illegal throughout the country. Do not test this—Britain has been cracking down on drug use for young people in particular over the past few years. Smoking is banned in enclosed public spaces in Britain, including pubs and restaurants.

Specific Concerns

Terrorism

The bombings of July 7, 2005 in the London Underground revealed the vulnerability of large European cities to terrorist attacks and resulted in the enforcement of stringent safety measures at airports and major tourist sights throughout British cities. Though seven years have passed, security checks are still as thorough as ever. Allow extra time for airport security and do not pack sharp objects in your carry-on luggage—they will be confiscated. Unattended luggage is always considered suspicious and is also liable to confiscation. Check your home country's foreign affairs office for travel information and advisories, and be sure to follow the local news while in the UK.

Pre-Departure Health

Matching a prescription to a foreign equivalent is not always easy, safe, or possible, so if you take **prescription drugs,** carry up-to-date prescriptions or a statement from your doctor stating the medications' trade names, manufacturers, chemical names, and dosages. Be sure to keep all medication with you in your carry-on luggage.

Immunizations and Precautions

Travelers over two years old should make sure that the following vaccines are up to date: MMR (for measles, mumps, and rubella); DTaP or Td (for diphtheria, tetanus, and pertussis); IPV (for polio); Hib (for *Haemophilus influenzae* B); and HepB (for Hepatitis B). For recommendations on immunizations and prophylaxis, check with a doctor and consult the **Centers for Disease Control and Prevention (CDC)** in the US (☎+1-800-232-4636; www.cdc.gov/travel) or the equivalent in your home country.

KEEPING IN TOUCH

By Email and Internet

Hello and welcome to the 21st century, where you're rarely more than a 5min. walk from the nearest Wi-Fi hot spot, even if sometimes you'll have to pay a few bucks or buy a drink for the privilege of using it. **Internet cafes** and free internet terminals are listed in the **Practicalities** section above. For lists of additional cybercafes in London check out www.cybercaptive.com.

Wireless hot spots make internet access possible in public and remote places. Unfortunately, they also pose security risks. Hot spots are public, open networks that use unencrypted, unsecured connections. They are susceptible to hacks and "packet sniffing"—the theft of passwords and other private information. To prevent problems, disable "ad hoc" mode, turn off file sharing and network discovery, encrypt your email, turn on your firewall, beware of phony networks, and watch for over-the-shoulder creeps.

By Telephone

Calling Home from London

If you have internet access, your best—i.e., cheapest, most convenient, and most tech-savvy—means of calling home is probably our good friend ▨Skype (www.skype.com). You can even videochat if you have one of those new-fangled webcams. Calls to other Skype users are free; calls to landlines and mobiles worldwide start at US$0.023 per minute, depending on where you're calling.

For those still stuck in the 20th century, **prepaid phone cards** are a common and relatively inexpensive means of calling abroad. Each one comes with a Personal Identification Number (PIN) and a toll-free access number. You call the access number and then follow the directions for dialing your PIN. To purchase prepaid phone cards, check online for the best rates; www.callingcards.com is a

Essentials

good place to start. Online providers generally send your access number and PIN via email, with no actual "card" involved. You can also call home with prepaid phone cards purchased in London.

Another option is a **calling card,** linked to a major national telecommunications service in your home country. Calls are billed collect or to your account. Cards generally come with instructions for dialing both domestically and internationally. Placing a collect call through an international operator can be expensive but may be necessary in case of an emergency. You can frequently call collect without even possessing a company's calling card just by calling its access number and following the instructions.

Sir Giles Gilbert Scott's swanky red-box phone booths still line the London streets. Adapted to the modern age, the public phone booths now accept both coins and cards. As with most former crown property, the price of modernization was privitization, with British Telecom now in charge of the operation and maintenance of these more modern, utilitarian boxes.

Cellular Phones

Cell phones are everywhere in the UK, although the Brits call them "mobile phones." Competitive, low prices and the variety of calling plans make them accessible even for short-term, low-budget travelers. For most visitors to the UK, a pay-as-you-go plan is the most attractive option. Pick up an eligible mobile (from £25) and recharge, or top up, with a card purchased at a grocery store, online, or by phone. Incoming calls and incoming text messages are always free. **Vodaphone** (www.vodaphone.co.uk) and **T-Mobile** (www.t-mobile.co.uk) are among the biggest providers. In other news, Britain has developed a huge text-messaging culture. We hope you have a gr8 time fitting in (lol).

By Snail Mail

Sending Mail Home From London

Airmail is the best way to send mail home from London. Write "airmail," on the front. For simple letters or postcards, airmail tends to be surprisingly cheap, but the price will go up sharply for weighty packages. Surface mail is by far the cheapest, slowest, and most antiquated way to send mail. It takes one to two months to cross the Atlantic and one to three to cross the Pacific—good for heavy items you won't need for a while, like souvenirs that you've acquired along the way.

Receiving Mail in London

There are several ways to arrange pickup of letters sent to you while you are in London even if you do not have an address of your own. Mail can be sent via **Poste Restante** (General Delivery) in English to London and it is pretty reliable. Address Poste Restante letters like so:

> Emma WATSON
> Poste Restante
> Trafalgar Square Post Office
> 24-28 William IV St.
> London, United Kingdom

London is a huge city, with many post offices. Try sending packages to the large and open-late Trafalgar Square Post Office. Bring your passport (or other photo ID) for pickup. If the clerks insist that there is nothing for you, ask them to check under your first name as well. It is usually safer and quicker, though more expensive, to send mail express or registered. If you don't want to deal with Poste Restante, consider asking your hostel or accommodation if you can have things mailed to you there. Of course, if you have your own mailing address or a reliable friend to receive mail for you, that will be the easiest solution.

TIME DIFFERENCES

Great Britain is on Greenwich Mean Time (GMT) and observes Daylight Saving Time. This means the Brits are 5hr. ahead of New York City and 8hr. ahead of Los Angeles. Note that Australia and New Zealand observe Daylight Saving Time from October to March, the opposite of the Northern Hemisphere—therefore, Sydney is 9hr. ahead of Britain from March to October and 11hr. ahead from October to March. Don't accidentally call your mom at 5am!

CLIMATE

We'd love to tell you that everything you've heard about British weather is false... but we're not here to lie to you. Britain is traditionally cool and summertime precipitation is considerably higher than other European destinations. Don't let the weather keep you from traveling to this wonderful country,

Essentials

but be prepared for some damp, chilly days during your stay. The silver lining is that there are few extremes either, so you're unlikely to melt, freeze, or be blown away by a freak storm during your trip.

MONTH	AVG. HIGH TEMP.		AVG. LOW TEMP.		AVG. RAINFALL		AVG. NUMBER OF WET DAYS
January	6°C	43°F	2°C	36°F	54mm	2.1 in.	15
February	7°C	45°F	2°C	36°F	40mm	1.6 in.	13
March	10°C	50°F	3°C	37°F	37mm	1.5 in.	11
April	13°C	55°F	6°C	43°F	37mm	1.5 in.	12
May	17°C	63°F	8°C	46°F	46mm	1.8 in.	12
June	20°C	68°F	12°C	54°F	45mm	1.8 in.	11
July	22°C	72°F	14°C	57°F	57mm	2.2 in.	12
August	21°C	70°F	13°C	55°F	59mm	2.3 in.	11
September	19°C	66°F	11°C	52°F	49mm	1.9 in.	13
October	14°C	57°F	8°C	46°F	57mm	2.2 in.	13
November	10°C	50°F	5°C	41°F	64mm	2.5 in.	15
December	7°C	45°F	4°C	39°F	48mm	1.9 in.	15

To convert from degrees Fahrenheit to degrees Celsius, subtract 32 and multiply by 5/9. To convert from Celsius to Fahrenheit, multiply by 9/5 and add 32. The mathematically challenged may use this handy chart:

°CELSIUS	-5	0	5	10	15	20	25	30	35	40
°FAHRENHEIT	23	32	41	50	59	68	77	86	95	104

MEASUREMENTS

Britain uses a thoroughly confusing and illogical mix of standard and metric measurement units. Road distances are always measured in miles, and many Brits will be clueless if you give them distances in kilometers. For weights, don't be surprised to see grams and ounces used side-by-side. There's also a measurement called a "stone," equal to 14 pounds, that is regularly used for giving body weights. Paradoxically, meters and centimeters are the most common way to give body heights. How the British ever accomplished anything in this world when they can't settle on a consistent system of measurements we'll never know. If you want to figure out whether you're buying enough pasta for one or for your entire hostel, use the chart below.

Essentials

MEASUREMENT CONVERSIONS	
1 inch (in.) = 25.4mm	1 millimeter (mm) = 0.039 in.
1 foot (ft.) = 0.305m	1 meter (m) = 3.28 ft.
1 yard (yd.) = 0.914m	1 meter (m) = 1.094 yd.
1 mile (mi.) = 1.609km	1 kilometer (km) = 0.621 mi.
1 ounce (oz.) = 28.35g	1 gram (g) = 0.035 oz.
1 pound (lb.) = 0.454kg	1 kilogram (kg) = 2.205 lb.
1 fluid ounce (fl. oz.) = 29.57mL	1 milliliter (mL) = 0.034 fl. oz.
1 gallon (gal.) = 3.785L	1 liter (L) = 0.264 gal.

London 101

From Westminster Abbey to Abbey Road, from the Queen of England to Elton John, from bangers 'n' mash to chicken tikka masala, London has something to satisfy every taste. To help you navigate through it all, London 101 is here to fill you in on the city's past and present. If the diversity of British food is overwhelming at first, don't fret, just check out the lowdown in our Food and Drink section. We'll also demystify the world of football without helmets and crickets that don't chirp in our Sports and Recreation section, and tell you when you should say "pissed" and shouldn't say "biggie" in Customs and Etiquette. Finally, we'll fill you in on all the Holidays and Festivals so you don't miss out on the Queen's Birthday festivities. Here we give you all the basics you need to make the most out of your London experience, whether it's three days or three months.

Facts and Figures

- **POPULATION:** 7,500,000
- **NUMBER OF JOHN SMITHS IN LONDON:** 30,000
- **TUBE STATIONS:** 270
- **UNIVERSITIES:** 43
- **MINUTES BIG BEN WAS SLOWED DOWN WHEN A FLOCK OF BIRDS LANDED ON THE MINUTE HAND IN 1945:** 5
- **NUMBER OF PEOPLE WHO LIVED IN THE UNDERGROUND DURING WWII:** 177,000

HISTORY

Legend has it that London was founded by Brutus of Troy, a descendant of Aeneas who was banished for accidentally killing his father. He then wandered across Europe, arrived in Britain, defeated the giants who lived there, and renamed the island after himself (Bru-tus, Bri-tain). If that sounds far-fetched, it's because it's a legend. But now you know.

Birthday (43-410 CE)

London was actually founded in 43 CE by the Romans (they called it **Londinium** then), just seven years after their conquest of Britain. It was meant to be a civilian town, as opposed to the military outposts the Romans had previously built in this restive northern frontier. Seventeen years later, the Celtic Warrior-Queen **Boudica** burned Londinium to the ground during her campaign to expel the Romans from her island. But the pesky foreigners came back and the town was rebuilt, now with city walls! (These old Roman walls still demarcate the historic **City of London** at the center of the now-sprawling metropolis.) The town grew in size and importance and became the capital of the Roman province of Britannia.

I Want You (She's So London) (410-1215)

In 410, after years of fighting British "barbarians," the Romans cleared out, in order to battle other "barbarians" (this time, of the German variety) on their home turf. Once the Romans were gone, Britain fell into a period of flux, with Saxons, Vikings, and Danes fighting over the city—until the Normans arrived in 1066 and showed everyone who was boss. **William the Conqueror,** who demolished his competitors for the crown at the **Battle of Hastings,** treated London with special attention. William transformed London into his capital by building three new castles (one of these is now known as the **Tower of London**).

Westminster, the enormous abbey that Edward the Confessor built just before the Normans took over, became the fiscal and legal center of the nation. London's status as the largest and wealthiest city in Britain made it a kingmaker in every disputed succession (trust us, there were a lot of these). Prospective monarchs had to make sure that they had London's support, or their heads would most likely end up on a pike.

Helter Skelter (1215-1666)

But political power doesn't make a city invincible. The city's densely-packed population and booming commerce made it highly susceptible to plagues and fires. The **Black Death** hit London in 1369 and killed more than half of the population. In 1665, the **Black Plague** reared its ugly head again and carried off about 100,000 Londoners. Then came the **Great Fire of 1666,** which leveled more than 60% of the city, including the original St. Paul's Cathedral and Royal Exchange. This time, many decided to rebuild in stone.

It's Getting Better All the Time (1666-1900)

In spite of its devastating destruction, the Great Fire helped make London the modern city it is today. Over the next 20 years, streets were widened, new stone houses were built, and the city began to assume the character of a modern metropolis. By the end of the 18th century, Samuel Johnson could say without a hint of irony, "when a man is tired of London, he is tired of life; for there is in London all that life can afford."

Despite losing its North American colonies in 1776, England became the most powerful country in the world. Having defeated France in the French-Indian and Napoleonic Wars, it was the ultimate colonial power. The spoils of its worldwide empire all poured back to London. Over the next century, **Big Ben** and the Houses of Parliament were built, the **National Gallery** was erected, a police force was established by Sir Robert Peel (hence the nicknames "bobbies and "peelers"), and a sewage system was put into place to spare Londoners a repeat of the **Greak Stink of 1858** (and prevent the cholera outbreaks that followed the habit of dumping an entire city's raw sewage in the Thames). The Underground, the first subterranean rail line in the world, opened in 1863. Within a few months, it was carrying more than 25,000 passengers a day.

The Industrial Revolution brought huge numbers of rural peasants to work in factories in the capital. London's population passed one million around 1800, and it remained the largest city in the world for much of the 19th century. By 1900, 6.7 million people called London home.

Magical Mystery Tour (1900-today)

Over the course of the 20th century, London survived two world wars, two Olympics, and Johnny Rotten. During WWII, German planes bombarded London in an eight-month **Blitz,** intended to terrorize Britons into submission. Beginning on September 7, 1940, the Luftwaffe bombed the city for 57 consecutive days. Children were evacuated, and more than 150,000 people camped out in the Underground each night. (The government explicitly forbade this practice, but people got around this by going to the extreme measure of…purchasing a ticket.) The Blitz destroyed more than a million houses, and left an enduring mark on the city.

But that didn't stop London from playing host to the world three years after the war ended with the first Olympics since the infamous Berlin games of 1936. In 1951, the Festival of Britain served as another much-needed celebration after the tough years of the war. It left behind the Royal Festival Hall, which has since evolved into the core of the South Bank's art complex. Vast housing projects made from prefabricated materials replaced the bombed-out streets, permitting more people than ever before to own their own flats.

By the 1960s, in the **Swinging London** period, the city really had its mojo back. Jean Shrimpton became one of the world's first supermodels, **the Beatles** ensconced themselves in Abbey Road Studios, **The Who's** Pete Townshend smashed up his guitar and shattered conventions, and hipsters were known as mods. It was a good time to be in London.

Since then, the city has only become more multi-ethnic, more artistic, and more tourist-friendly. In 2000, Ken Livingstone—a man who said, "If voting changed anything, they'd abolish it"— became London's first elected mayor. Under his watch, London won its bid to host the 2012 Olympics (see **Arts and Culture**), introduced a motorist fee to cut down on congestion in the city, and gave the Underground a facelift. Though riots in the summer of 2011 were a symbol of the difficult times faced by post-economic crisis Britain, the city's residents roundly rejected the anarchy of the rioters and pulled together to reassert their community. Now London excitedly prepares for its third Olympics, an honor no city has ever received before.

CUSTOMS AND ETIQUETTE

Brits and Americans may both speak English, but that doesn't mean that they can always understand each other. As George Bernard Shaw once remarked, "America and Britain are two nations separated by a common language." Here are some phrases you should know not to mix up:

- **BIGGIE:** Carries the double-meaning of "doo-doo," what a child calls number two, and an erection. Watch out, the reflexive "no biggie" could take on a whole new world of significance.

- **BLOW ME:** Not the euphemism that we're used to, it's merely an exclamation of surprise in this land.

- **BLOW OFF:** To fart.

- **FAGS:** Not a gay slur, but merely cigarettes.

- **FOOTBALL:** There are no touchdowns or field goals in this game. Remember, don't talk about "soccer" here, or you might bring the wrath of legendary football hardman Vinnie Jones upon you.

- **PISSED:** Means drunk, not angry.

- **SEPTIC (TANK):** Rhyming Cockney slang for yank (as in American).

While we're at it, here's a short guide to some other English slang worth knowing:

- **ACE:** Cool or awesome.

- **AGGRO:** Short for aggravation.

- **ALL RIGHT?:** Used a lot around London and the south to mean, "Hello, how are you?"

- **BARMY:** If someone tells you that you're barmy, they mean you have gone mad or crazy (e.g. you'd have to be barmy to visit England without trying black pudding).

- **BELT UP:** Shut up.

- **BLADDERED:** A rather disgusting way to say someone is drunk.

- **COCK UP:** A mistake.

All in the (Royal) Family

In London, you never know when you might run into royalty, so it doesn't hurt to be prepared to recognize any eligible young princes or princesses. Here's a quick rundown of the most important royals:

- **QUEEN ELIZABETH II.** Queen since 1952, this lovely lady is the second longest-reigning monarch in British history. She'll be celebrating her Diamond Jubilee the first weekend of June 2012, so expect patriotic concerts and parades.

- **PRINCE PHILIP.** Elizabeth's husband and consort. Renowned for his lack of tact, he once told some British students in China, "If you stay here much longer, you'll be all slitty-eyed."

- **PRINCE CHARLES.** The Prince of Wales, he is the first in line to the throne.

- **PRINCE WILLIAM.** Second in line to the throne after his father, he recently married his sweetheart Lady Catherine Middleton and spends most of his time proving his manliness by serving with the Royal Air Force in Wales.

- **PRINCE HARRY.** The second son of Prince Charles and Princess Diana, this scoundrel is finally beginning to grow up, but he's still on the market for a wife. Any takers?

- **CHEESED OFF:** A British equivalent of "pissed off."

- **DEKKO:** Borrowed from Hindi, this means to take a look at something.

FOOD AND DRINK

British food often gets a bad rap, probably because of English favorites with names like jellied eel and spotted dick. But many traditional standards are actually quite delicious, and no visit to London is complete without sampling some fish 'n' chips, Yorkshire pudding (fried batter), or bangers and mash (sausage and mashed potatoes).

In your English travels, you're almost certain to find a **"full breakfast"** (eggs, sausage, beans, fried tomato, and buttered toast) or a **"ploughman's lunch"** (cheese, onions, pickles, and a hunk of bread) at any pub. The customary **tea** takes place between three and five in the afternoon. Head to a hotel lobby or a sit-down cafe and they'll surely have cucumber sandwiches and scones with clotted cream and jam, not to mention the actual namesake beverage.

One of the advantages of having a global empire was the ability to pick and choose all the best foods the world had to offer. Even with the empire gone, London is still an international city, and its food reflects that. **Chicken tikka masala** has become, by some accounts, the most popular English dish. (Chicken tikka is an Indian dish to which cooks added gravy to satisfy the British desire for meat with gravy. In 2001, the UK's Foreign Secretary, Robin Cook, proclaimed it "a true British national dish," calling it "a perfect illustration of the way Britain absorbs and adapts external influences.")

The sun has long since set on the days when sandwich meant two pieces of Wonderbread, some mayo, and a thin piece of meat. Now, you're more likely to find yourself being treated to a Vietnamese *bánh mì* or a Middle Eastern falafel. South Asian curries, Caribbean *roti,* Chinese dim sum, Spanish paella, and everything in between can be found on London's streets.

SPORTS AND RECREATION

Football

Soccer is king here, but don't call it that: **football** rules the roost. The English boast that the game was created here and whether that's true or not, they certainly act as if it is. Pubs are packed every Saturday and Sunday as football supporters (not fans) gather to cheer for their favorite team in the domestic leagues: the **Premiership,** the **Championship, League 1,** and **League 2.** Pubs are packed again on midweek evenings as the supporters of those lucky seven clubs that made the European leagues cheer on their teams' charge for continental glory. London itself currently boasts five teams in the top flight (the Premiership): Arsenal, Chelsea, Fulham, Queens Park Rangers, and Tottenham. However, the passion felt for the clubs is nothing compared with how people feel about the national team: **the Three Lions.** The football team is perpetually star-crossed, but, despite its constant surfeit of incredible talent, it has not won the World Cup since 1966; the team always seems to do just well enough to cause national heartbreak each time they lose in spectacular fashion.

Cricket

For those not of the footy persuasion, there's **cricket,** a game that we yanks just don't get. There's a pitcher (who they call a **bowler**), a batter (sorry, a **batsman**), and innings (one or two depending on the game). Beyond that it all gets rather opaque. It's like a longer, slower version of baseball—games can last up to five days!—if the creator of baseball had gotten bladdered at the pub and thought two batsmen running between two wickets was equivalent to rounding the bases and that it was a good idea to have a position called "Silly Mid-Off."

HOLIDAYS AND FESTIVALS

HOLIDAY OR FESTIVAL	DESCRIPTION	DATE
London International Mime Festival	So much silence. But really, it's a gathering of more mimes than you'll see in the rest of your life. Check out the theatres or www.mimefest.co.uk to see what those silent actors have gotten up to.	January 14-29, 2012
Pancake Day	Shrove Tuesday (sometimes known as Mardi Gras)is celebrated throughout Britain with the eating of delicious crepe-like creations and so-called "Pancake races," where competitors sprint while flipping pancakes in pans.	February 21, 2012
St. George's Day	England's national day, celebrating the country's favorite dragon-slaying saint.	April 23
The Queen's Diamond Jubilee	Queen Elizabeth II celebrates 60 years on the throne in this Commonwealth-wide party. Many events are planned, including a concert, street parties, and a boat parade on the Thames.	June 5, 2012 (this year only!)
The Queen's Birthday	Official holiday celebrating the Queen's birthday, even though her real birthday is months earlier. It's the biggest royal event of the year. The parade takes place in Whitehall, accessible from the tube stop at Westminster.	June 9, 2012
Notting Hill Carnival	Billing itself as "the biggest carnival in Europe," this extravaganza looks to show off the biggest and craziest floats ever when it takes the world stage in 2012, sandwiched in between the Olympics and Paralympics.	August 26-27, 2012
Lord Mayor's Show and Fireworks Display	A HUGE fireworks show that has been put on hold only for the Black Death and the Duke of Wellington's funeral. Otherwise it's been happening annually since 1215.	November 10, 2012
Christmas	You know the deal: Christmas tree, baby Jesus, presents—except in England they actually eat mincemeat pies and fruitcake.	December 25
Boxing Day	The day after Christmas is the British equivalent of Black Friday. Everybody rushes to the stores and spends their Christmas cash on deeply discounted goodies.	December 26

Beyond Tourism

If you are reading this, then you are a member of an elite group—and we don't mean "the literate." You're a student preparing for a semester abroad. You're taking a gap year to save the trees, the whales, or the dates. You're an 80-year-old woman who has devoted her life to egg-laying platypuses and what the hell is up with that. In short, you're a traveler, not a tourist; like any good spy, you don't just observe your surroundings—you become an active part of them.

Your mission, should you choose to accept it, is to study, volunteer, or work abroad as laid out in the dossier—er, chapter—below. We leave the rest (when to go, whom to bring, and how many Arrested Development DVDs to pack) in your hands. This message will self-destruct in five seconds. Good luck.

STUDYING

Sure, you could take a break from school and spend countless hours eating fish and chips or watching the changing of the guard—*or* you could put that brain of yours to good use and let the Brits teach you something new. With dozens of world-renowned universities to choose from, it shouldn't be any problem finding some classes that spark your interest and have you swotting (or studying) in no time.

Visa Information

Citizens of the United States who plan to study in the United Kingdom for less than six months can enter as a student visitor without a visa. If you plan on staying longer than six months, you will need a **Tier 4 Visa.** In order to apply for a visa, you will need to provide an application form, a letter of acceptance to a course or university, proof that you have sufficient financial resources to support yourself during your stay, and an application fee of £220. Applications for a visa may be submitted online or through the nearest British consulate. Visa applications can take up to 60 days to be processed, so arrange your paperwork well in advance. Student visa holders are not allowed to work during their stay in the UK. We recommend checking **www. ukvisas.gov.uk** for the most current information and a detailed guide to the application process.

Universities

Many schools are located in Central London and are easy to get to from local bachelor pads. You can take classes on a variety of topics, from economics to literature and art history. You may be zonked from working hard, but hey, at least all the classes are in English.

The London School of Economics and Political Science (LSE)

Houghton St.

☎020 7405 7686; www.lse.ac.uk

Arcadia University (+1-866-927-2234; www.arcadia.edu/abroad) offers a year-long academic program at the famous LSE. You choose four year-long courses at the central London campus. The school is obviously renowned for social sciences, but offers instruction in a wide variety of subjects.

▸ *i* 3.3 GPA required.

Royal Holloway

Egham Hill, Egham

☎01784 434 455; www.rhul.ac.uk

Part of the University of London, Royal Holloway offers semester- and year-long programs for study-abroad students, and is known for theater, music, psychology, geography, English literature, and history.

▸ *i* 3.0 GPA required.

University College London (UCL)

32 Russell Sq.

☎020 7679 2000; www.ucl.ac.uk

One of the world's top universities, UCL is located in the heart of Central London, adjacent to the British Museum. Students choose four courses per semester out of a pool of tutorials, lectures, and even one-on-one classes. The university helps students find housing in either intercollegiate halls or private apartments.

City University

Northampton Sq.

☎020 7040 5060; www.city.ac.uk

City University is a large, urban university with a substantial international community. Classes are offered in business, engineering, journalism, politics, psychology, sociology, and more.

▸ *i* 4-6 courses per semester. [$] Semester £3815; year £11,500.

The Arts

From the Royal Shakespeare Company to the Rolling Stones, London has been home to some of the world's greatest artists. It may just be the perfect place to focus your creative energy as well.

American Institute for Foreign Study (AIFS)

River Plaza, 9 W. Broad St., Stamford, CT 06902, USA

☎+1-800-727-2437; www.aifsabroad.com

You can continue your American education across the pond with AIFS's semester-long programs at Richmond, The American International University in London. The real gem of AIFS's offerings, though, may be the chance to unlock your inner

Mercutio at their three-week course in movement, voice, and scene rehearsals at Shakespeare's Globe Theatre.

▶ *i* Min. 2.5 GPA. Ⓢ Semester $15,995; summer $5500-11,000; Globe program $5795.

Courtauld Institute of Art

Somerset House, Strand

☎020 7872 0220; www.courtald.ac.uk

Based out of central London's Somerset House, the Courtauld Institute of Art is known for both its remarkable painting collection and its challenging art history courses. The Institute is affiliated with the University of London, so some students take classes there as well.

▶ *i* Min. 3.5 GPA.

Royal Academy of Music

Marylebone Rd.

☎020 7873 7373; www.ram.ac.uk

An exchange program offered through the University of Miami (☎+1-305-284-3434; www.miami.edu/index.php/study _abroad) allows students to study at one of Britain's most renowned conservatories, home to 650 students from over 50 countries. The year-long program will keep you busy with lessons, concerts, operas, and musical theater as you learn about instrumental performance and composition.

▶ *i* Many students stay in residence halls at the University of London.

VOLUNTEERING

So you're thinking it's about time to get off your arse and get your hands dirty doing some volunteer work? Well, we here at Let's Go think that's a bloody good idea. From going green to raising green, from saving the habitat of furry woodland animals to helping disadvantaged kids, London can help you help others. So chivvy along, get out there, and do some good for the world.

Environmental Conservation

Go London

237 Pentonville Rd.

☎020 7643 1373; www.csv.org.uk

GO London is an environmental volunteer organization that

requires little commitment for those just looking to volunteer for a couple of days while staying in the city. Typical volunteers work on city farms, clean up rubbish, and plant gardens. If you're looking for more of a long-term commitment, you can become a GO event leader. The organization will train and then assign you a volunteer group and a project to work on.

▶ *i* No experience required. Ages 16+.

Wildlife For All

The Oasis, Highbrook Lane, West Hoathly, Sussex
☎07946 313 718; www.wildlifeforall.org

With Wildlife for All, you can volunteer to help run The Oasis, a nature reserve and education center about 30 mi. south of London. No experience is necessary, but know that they expect very serious and highly committed volunteers.

Greenpeace

Canonbury Villas
☎020 7865 8100; www.greenpeace.org.uk

Volunteers for Greenpeace in London help protect the environment by working on marketing, supporter services, campaigns, policy and solutions, media, web, publications, human resources, or reception and information systems.

Global Issues

People and Planet

51 Union St., Oxford
☎01865 245 678; www.peopleandplanet.org

People and Planet, an organization fighting world poverty and hunger, needs volunteers at festivals throughout the year. Check their website for availability.

Youth Issues

Alone in London

Unit 6, 48 Provost St.
☎020 7447 3192; www.aloneinlondon.org

This organization strives to prevent homelessness by supporting at-risk young people. As a volunteer, you can provide a welcoming and safe environment to youths, offering advice and support. Alone in London runs training for all its volunteers.

All About Kids

Stafford House, 91 Keymer Rd., Hassocks, West Sussex

☎01273 847 770; www.cchf-allaboutkids.org

As an Activity Break Volunteer, you will work with disadvantaged kids, listening, mentoring, and supporting them and leading them in singing, dancing, and other fun activities.

▶ *i* Must be able to commit to 6 consecutive days or 2 weekends throughout the year. Training included.

Activism

amnesty international

1 Easton St.

☎020 7413 5500; www.amnesty.org

You can help Amnesty International in London by monitoring the international press, translating, undertaking research, designing web pages, raising funds, and supporting human resources and accounting.

Trade Justice Movement

www.tjm.org.uk

Trade Justice Movement works with numerous other organizations to fight the harmful effects of trade rules on the impoverished, the environment, and democracy.

WORKING

If you've run out of money and need to replenish that wallet without begging the parentals for financial aid, stop lazing around and ring a few of our listings to set up an interview.

Long-Term Work

Teaching

Unlike most other international destinations, London doesn't have much demand for English teachers. Other teaching jobs are also difficult to find, because many sectors do not hire non-British citizens.

However, some schools are willing to hire American college graduates and offer them free on-the-job training. There are also several services that can help you find positions as a personal tutor.

UK Tutors

www.uktutors.com

Through the UK Tutors website, you can register yourself as a personal tutor and advertise to prospective employers. Think Match.com, except instead of an awkward date, you get a job out of it.

TES Connect

26 Red Lion Sq.

☎020 3194 3000; www.tes.co.uk

TES Connect is a resource for finding open teaching jobs. Through this site, you can find schools willing to hire uncertified teachers, though you must be a college graduate to qualify.

My Private Tutor

4 Gregory Close, Lower Earley, Reading, Berkshire

www.myprivatetutor.org.uk

My Private Tutor is another company that lets you register for free to become a personal tutor (but to see their full database of students you have to pay extra). Their site asks you to make a profile listing your qualifications, allows students in your area of the city to find you, and gives you the freedom to set your own fees.

Au Pair Work

A Class Au Pairs

60 Winchester Ave., Upminster, Essex

☎01708 250 976; www.aclassaupairs.co.uk

A Class places au pairs with families throughout London. The organization requires that applicants register with the police, be between 18 and 27, single, and have no dependents.

► $ Average salary £55 per week.

Cinderella Au Pairs

291 Kirkdale, Sydenham

☎020 8659 1689; www.cinderellaaupairs.co.uk

This agency places au pairs throughout London and Great Britain. You will be expected to complete regular au pair work but may also receive more flexibility and time off than you'd expect.

▶ Ⓢ Salary approx. £55 per week. *i* Min. stay 3 months for a summer placement; 6-12 months for other placements.

Astor International
3 Croxford Gardens
☎020 8888 8144; www.aaupair.co.uk

Astor is an international au pair and nanny agency based in the UK. Register online and be matched with a family in London after a security check, interview, and short test.

Peek-A-Boo
14 King St., 5th fl.
☎020 7600 9880; www.peekaboochildcare.com

Peek-A-Boo pairs prospective au pairs with families and provides social interactions for their au pairs, including monthly pub nights, parties, trips, and discounts on entry tickets to UK attractions.

▶ Ⓢ Average salary £70 per week.

More Visa Information

If you plan to work in the United Kingdom for less than six months, you will need a work permit but not a visa. If you plan to work longer than that, you will need two documents: a **visa** and a **Certificate of Sponsorship.** Skilled workers apply for a Tier 2 visa, while temporary workers need a Tier 5 visa. Those who wish to work as investors, entrepreneurs, or are doing post-study work, must apply for a Tier 1 visa.

The Certificate of Sponsorship is a document with information on both you and your employer. A VAF9 form, with your personal information and a PBS Appendix Form that corresponds to the tier of visa you apply for, must be submitted along with your passport, visa fee, biometric details, and a recent passport-sized photograph. You must also demonstrate that you have sufficient funds (£800 per month) to support yourself while in the UK.

The temporary worker visa costs £130, and is valid for one year. Most visas are processed within 60 days. You can apply online at www.visa4uk.fco.gov.uk, through a Visa Application Center, or at your country's British consulate.

Internships

Parliament

☎+1-215-572-2901; www.arcadia.edu/abroad

Get an in-depth look at British politics through Arcadia University's Parliamentary Internship program. As an intern, you will attend meetings, conferences, events, and special sessions with your favorite Parliamentarians. Along with interning three days per week, participants take two classes and complete a research paper.

▸ *i* Semester-long program. Min. 3.2 GPA. $ $14,900

Greenpeace

www.greenpeace.org.uk

Getting a foothold in the environmental sector can be difficult, so Greenpeace offers a number of internships in their London office to get started. This is a good place to look if you're hoping to develop skills and experience in environmental activism.

▸ *i* Min. 1 month commitment. $ Unpaid.

Short-Term Work

Short-term job openings are always changing. If you're looking to find an easy job with little long-term commitment, or looking to make some fast cash to keep the party going, try searching on internet job databases, in local newspapers, or in business windows for "Now Hiring" signs.

Just Jobs 4 Students

1 Canada Sq.

☎0845 468 0568; www.justjobs4students.co.uk

Just Jobs 4 Students is a job search engine reserved for students. Its outlook on the job hunting process is made clear by its asking you not what job you want but what you can "cope with." You can find jobs like housekeeping, receptionist, sales assistant, fundraising, and more.

Live-In Jobs

☎01764 670 001; www.livein-jobs.co.uk

Live-In jobs sets you up with seasonal work in hotels in exchange for room and board. Travelers often work as waiters, bartenders, housekeepers, receptionists, and even chefs.

▸ *i* 3-6 month commitment.

Season Workers

☎0845 643 9338; www.seasonworkers.com

Season Workers will help you find work at resorts and camps across Britain during the summer. Many jobs on this site provide competitive wages, accommodation, and food.

Worlk Wide Opportunities on Organic Farms (wwoof)

www.wwoof.org.uk

WWOOF gives a list of organic farms, gardens, and smallholdings in the UK that offer room and board in exchange for help. You are not expected to have any previous agricultural experience.

▶ $ Member fee £20.

Tell the World

If your friends are tired of hearing about that time you saved a baby orangutan in Indonesia, there's clearly only one thing to do: get new friends. Find them at our website, www.letsgo.com, where you can post your study-, volunteer-, or work-abroad stories for other, more appreciative community members to read.

Index

Accommodations Index

Restaurants Index

Nightlife Index

Shopping Index

LONDON ACKNOWLEDGMENTS

SPENCER THANKS: To Linda for fomenting revolution. To Kat, Nicole, Beebs, and RoRo for risking life and limb to bring us intrepid reporting, sterling research, and rib-cracking marginalia. To the legendary sass of Billy and Michael. To Chris for keeping us on shedule. To Iya for being the second most famous Georgian I know. To trivia for simultaneously improving and decimating my self-esteem. To the Red-Headed League. To Proletariat Coffee (and capitalist coffee too). To Electric Ladyland. To Kentucky's finest bourbon, to Cambridge summers and porch-sitting, to Jack Spicer. To CuddlePod, Animal Farm, Whitney's tattoo artistry, Joe's futon, venn diagrams, the office snuggie, headgear of oracular origins, and sleep. To my parents. And most of all to Tanjore Tuesdays for fueling LGHQ through a long, hot summer.

LINDA THANKS: The cause for meaning. The Frevolution and those classy Tuesday nights. Israel, for being Israel. Amy for sanity. Michael for adorableness. Mp styles for sweet jamz and leading the charge. Billy for conducting the chorus of wahh. Spencer for the glory and the primates and the cuddles. Beatrice for being great. TWiz Khalifa because he deserves a thumbpick somewhere. That man at Dunks for not making me explain myself. All Comrades, all around the world, we salute you. JTR.

ABOUT LET'S GO

The Student Travel Guide

Let's Go publishes the world's favorite student travel guides, written entirely by Harvard students. Armed with pens, notebooks, and a few changes of clothes stuffed into their backpacks, our student researchers go across continents, through time zones, and above expectations to seek out invaluable travel experiences for our readers. Because we are a completely student-run company, we have a unique perspective on how students travel, where they want to go, and what they're looking to do when they get there. If your dream is to grab a machete and forge through the jungles of Costa Rica, we can take you there. If you'd rather bask in the Riviera sun at a beachside cafe, we'll set you a table. In short, we write for readers who know that there's more to travel than tour buses. To keep up, visit our website, www.letsgo.com, where you can sign up to blog, post photos from your trips, and connect with the Let's Go community.

Traveling Beyond Tourism

We're on a mission to provide our readers with sharp, fresh coverage packed with socially responsible opportunities to go beyond tourism. Each guide's Beyond Tourism chapter shares ideas about responsible travel, study abroad, and how to give back to the places you visit while on the road. To help you gain a deeper connection with the places you travel, our fearless researchers scour the globe to give you the heads-up on both world-renowned and off-the-beaten-track opportunities. We've also opened our pages to respected writers and scholars to hear their takes on the countries and regions we cover, and asked travelers who have worked, studied, or volunteered abroad to contribute first-person accounts of their experiences.

Fifty-Two Years of Wisdom

Let's Go has been on the road for 52 years and counting. We've grown a lot since publishing our first 20-page pamphlet to Europe in 1960, but five decades and 60 titles later, our witty, candid guides are still researched and written entirely by students on shoestring budgets who know that train strikes, stolen luggage, food poisoning, and marriage proposals are all part of a day's work. Meanwhile, we're still bringing readers fresh new features, such as a student-life section with advice on how and where to meet students from around the world; a revamped, user-friendly layout for our listings; and greater emphasis on the experiences that make travel abroad a rite of passage for readers of all ages. And, of course, this year's 16 titles—including five brand-new guides—are still brimming with editorial honesty, a commitment to students, and our irreverent style.

The Let's Go Community

More than just a travel guide company, Let's Go is a community that reaches from our headquarters in Cambridge, MA, all across the globe. Our small staff of dedicated student editors, writers, and tech nerds comes together because of our shared passion for travel and our desire to help other travelers get the most out of their experience. We love it when our readers become part of the Let's Go community as well—when you travel, drop us a postcard (67 Mt. Auburn St., Cambridge, MA 02138, USA), send us an email (feedback@letsgo.com), or sign up on our website (www. letsgo.com) to tell us about your adventures and discoveries.

For more information, updated travel coverage, and news from our researcher team, visit us online at www.letsgo.com.

LET'S GO BUDGET

TAKE A LET'S GO BUDGET GUIDE TO EUROPE

LET'S GO BUDGET AMSTERDAM
978-1-61237-015-6

LET'S GO BUDGET ATHENS
978-1-61237-005-7

LET'S GO BUDGET BARCELONA
978-1-61237-014-9

LET'S GO BUDGET BERLIN
978-1-61237-006-4

LET'S GO BUDGET FLORENCE
978-1-61237-007-1

LET'S GO BUDGET ISTANBUL
978-1-61237-008-8

LET'S GO BUDGET LONDON
978-1-61237-013-2

LET'S GO BUDGET MADRID
978-1-61237-009-5

LET'S GO BUDGET PARIS
978-1-61237-011-8

LET'S GO BUDGET PRAGUE
978-1-61237-010-1

LET'S GO BUDGET ROME
978-1-61237-012-5

ALL LET'S GO BUDGET GUIDEBOOKS ARE $9.99.
*Let's Go also publishes guides to individual countries
that are available at bookstores and online retailers.*

For more information: visit **LETSGO.COM**
JOIN THE DISCUSSION WITH LET'S GO ON **FACEBOOK** AND **TWITTE**

HELPING LET'S GO. If you want to share your discoveries, suggestions, or corrections, please drop us a line. We appreciate every piece of correspondence, whether a postcard, a 10-page email, or a coconut. Visit Let's Go at www.letsgo. com or send an email to:

feedback@letsgo.com, subject: "Let's Go Budget London"

Address mail to:

Let's Go Budget London, 67 Mount Auburn St., Cambridge, MA 02138, USA

In addition to the invaluable travel advice our readers share with us, many are kind enough to offer their services as researchers or editors. Unfortunately, our charter enables us to employ only currently enrolled Harvard students.
Maps © Let's Go and Avalon Travel
Interior design by Darren Alessi
Production by Amber Pirker
Photos © Let's Go, Beatrice Franklin and Benjamin Naddaff-Hafrey, photographers

Distributed by Publishers Group West.
Printed in Canada by Friesens Corp.

ISBN-13: 978-1-61237-013-2
ISBN-10: 1-61237-013-6
First edition
10 9 8 7 6 5 4 3 2 1

Let's Go Budget London is written by Let's Go Publications, 67 Mt. Auburn St., Cambridge, MA 02138, USA.

Let's Go® and the LG logo are trademarks of Let's Go, Inc.

QUICK REFERENCE

YOUR GUIDE TO LET'S GO ICONS

🖥	Let's Go recommends	☎	Phone numbers	🕂	Directions
i	Other hard info	Ⓢ	Prices	🕐	Hours

IMPORTANT PHONE NUMBERS

EMERGENCY: ☎112			
Amsterdam	☎911	London	☎999
Barcelona	☎092	Madrid	☎092
Berlin	☎110	Paris	☎17
Florence	☎113	Prague	☎158
Istanbul	☎155	Rome	☎113

USEFUL PHRASES

ENGLISH	FRENCH	GERMAN	ITALIAN	SPANISH
Hello/Hi	Bonjour/Salut	Hallo/Tag	Ciao	Hola
Goodbye/Bye	Au revoir	Auf Wiedersehen/ Tschüss	Arrivederci/Ciao	Adios/Chao
Yes	Oui	Ja	Sì	Sí
No	Non	Nein	No	No
Excuse me!	Pardon!	Entschuldigen Sie!	Scusa!	Perdón!
Thank you	Merci	Danke	Grazie	Gracias
Go away!	Va t'en!	Geh weg!	Vattene via!	Vete!
Help!	Au secours!	Hilfe!	Aiuto!	Ayuda!
Call the police!	Appelez la police!	Ruf die Polizei!	Chiamare la polizia!	Llame a la policía!
Get a doctor!	Cherchez un médecin!	Hol einen Arzt!	Avere un medico!	Llame a un médico!
I don't understand	Je ne comprends pas	Ich verstehe nicht	Non capisco	No comprendo
Do you speak English?	Parlez-vous anglais?	Sprechen Sie Englisch?	Parli inglese?	¿Habla inglés?
Where is...?	Où est...?	Wo ist...?	Dove...?	¿Dónde está...?

TEMPERATURE CONVERSIONS

°CELSIUS	-5	0	5	10	15	20	25	30	35	40
°FAHRENHEIT	23	32	41	50	59	68	77	86	95	104

MEASUREMENT CONVERSIONS

1 inch (in.) = 25.4mm	1 millimeter (mm) = 0.039 in.
1 foot (ft.) = 0.305m	1 meter (m) = 3.28 ft.
1 mile (mi.) = 1.609km	1 kilometer (km) = 0.621 mi.
1 pound (lb.) = 0.454kg	1 kilogram (kg) = 2.205 lb.
1 gallon (gal.) = 3.785L	1 liter (L) = 0.264 gal.